T0168995

THE TUDOR COOKBOOK
FROM GILDED PEACOCK TO CALVES' FEET PIE

THE TUDOR COOKBOOK
FROM GILDED PEACOCK TO CALVES' FEET PIE

TERRY BREVERTON

AMBERLEY

This edition published 2019

Amberley Publishing
The Hill, Stroud
Gloucestershire, GL5 4EP

www.amberley-books.com

British Library Cataloguing in Publication Data.
A catalogue record for this book is available from the British Library.

ISBN 978 1 4456 8943 2 (paperback)
ISBN 978 1 4456 4903 0 (ebook)

Typesetting and Origination by Amberley Publishing.
Printed in the UK.

Contents

Introduction

This is a splendid starting point for the adventurous cook, or one who wishes to experiment with very different dishes which seem surprisingly modern, with a real mix of savoury and sweet in the same dish. Nearly all of the recipes have been experimented with by modern practitioners and enthusiasts, and one can check online modern redactions of them. A list of some of the main online sources can be found in at the back of the book. Nearly all of the recipes have been taken from books written within the Tudor era of 1485 to 1603, but dishes from a few early seventeenth-century books have also been included as they include recipes dating from the sixteenth century. I have tried to largely omit dishes included in my far more extensive companion volume, *The Tudor Kitchen: What the Tudors Ate and Drank*.

The aforementioned book included recipes from the Plantagenet and Stuart eras that were known to have been used in Tudor times, but this work attempts to avoid any replication. In this work, no attempt is made to update the recipes for today's cook; the ingredients and quantities are included, and often cooking times, but it is up to the reader to try and replicate the dishes. Interpretation of quantities has generally been omitted unless they are specifically given. We must remember that most cooking was carried out in pots or on spits over an open fire, and that meat, fish and vegetables were often cooked in hard pastry containers which might then be thrown away or given to the poor.

Some archaic words, like *paste* to mean pastry, have been altered. Recipes might say 'do faire water into a pot' or 'take faire water', which means add fresh water, and often *hem* means them and *hit* means it – meanings that have been amended accordingly. To translate the dishes into modern English would lose much of the language of the times, and reduce enjoyment in the reading. I have only changed the language of the recipes insofar as to make them intelligible to the modern reader, for instance replacing *serue* with serve, *vpon* with upon, *iuice* with juice, *feason* with season, and *euery* with every, for example. Many of the longer sentences have been divided to make better sense, with new punctuation, but as much as possible I have tried to keep to the spirit of the originals, merely attempting to make them more easily readable. There was no standardised spelling at this time, nor dictionaries, and one can see that spellings vary even within the sample recipe below, which has been reproduced as exactly as possible. In *Gentyll Manly Cokere*, MS Pepys 1047, of around 1490, the translation of the handwritten manuscript is:

To make a stew of flesh yf thy potte be iiij gallons do yn A quarte of wyn take fayre befe of the fore loyne or of the hynder loyne and mynsitt and take gode Capons with all Take pepur and gode poder of Cannell and gyngere and rasyns of Corance clowse maces saferon & saunders take þer to onyons percelly sage Rosemary tyme ysope saffery hony clarefyed and a quantite of bryssyd Almondys and put ther to and boyll hit vp but thow nedys to have A fayre of colys for byrnyng And not to grete A fyre but small sokyng fyre And sokyd well in þe stewyng And loke thy pott be well keverd that the hete go not owte in no wyse And thus stew all maner flesh.

My 'modernised' version, to reduce confusion, is:

To make a stew of flesh. If thy pot be 4 gallons, add in a quart of wine. Add fair beef of the foreloin or of the hind loin and mince it, and add good capons [castrated cockerels or large chickens]. Take pepper, good powder of canell [the herb *canella*, similar to cinnamon], ginger, raisins of Corance [Corinth raisins are currants], cloves, mace, saffron & saunders [sandalwood]. Add thereto onions, parsley, sage, rosemary, thyme, hyssop, savory, clarified honey, and a quantity [large amount] of bruised almonds. Bring to the boil, but you need to have a coal fire [probably charcoal] for burning, and not too great a fire but a small good for boiling fyre. And boil well in the stewing. And take care your pot is well covered, so the heat does not escape. And thus stew all manner of meat.

1. The marriage feast of Sir Henry Unton, an English diplomat of the Elizabethan era, from around 1596. There would be various entertainments between and during courses.

1

What the Tudors Ate

Many Tudor dishes were served on sops (or soppes, or sippets), pieces of bread or toast, necessary carbohydrates before the later adoption of potatoes. The Tudors had some wonderful flavour combinations which are only now being appreciated, especially the mixing of sweet and savoury. Of course, nearly all these surviving recipes were for the richer classes – the poor had a monotonous diet of pottages or gruel with little meat. There are relatively few dishes for beef – it was a rich man's dish, generally roasted, and thus needing no recipes. Mutton was only eaten at the end of the sheep's useful life bearing lambs and supplying wool, and Tudor sheep were about a third of today's size. Veal, venison and wild boar were the most prized meats, but the rich also ate pork, lamb, mutton, beef and game, such as hare or rabbit. A wide range of wildfowl was eaten, along with pigeon and, at feasts, pheasant, partridge and even peacock and swan.

Fresh meat was hung in cool larders. It cost too much to feed animals other than sheep in winter, so most were killed in the autumn and their meat put in salt barrels, which removed the moisture and prevented bacterial growth. Before cooking, this salted meat was soaked many times but it never completely lost its saltiness. If soaked for a long time then most of the salt would be removed, but so would the flavour of the meat, making it almost tasteless. Fish was preserved in the same way. Foods were cooked by boiling, roasting or baking. Meat was boiled or cooked on a spit over fire. Soup, broth or pottage was cooked over an open fire and bread, pies and pastries were baked in simple brick ovens. Fires were lit in the ovens and, when the temperature was right, the ashes were raked out, the food placed in and the oven sealed.

Food was a status symbol, and the rich often ate three good meals a day, each made up of a number of courses. During the period there was a gradual change from serving meals in trenchers – dishes made of bread – to serving in wooden bowls. Each course contained a variety of dishes from which the guests could choose. They were all placed on the table at the same time. People ate with knives, spoons or their fingers. You had to bring your own cutlery, as this was not provided. Spoons, in particular, were highly prized status symbols. Indeed, the more expensive the spoon, the higher up in society you were. Forks were introduced from Italy during Henry VIII's reign but they were used mainly for serving rather than eating. The usual practice was to pick a little of each dish, for instance lifting a piece of meat onto your trencher. In essence, the rich man's table was a little like today's dim sum, tapas or thali meals, picking little bits of what you fancy over an extended period. Any unwanted parts of bone or gristle were cut away and placed in a 'voider', probably to be used as a stock base. The meat was then dipped into a relevant sauce. Leftovers were given to servants or the poor – nothing was wasted.

A common misconception is that spices were used to disguise the taste of meat that had gone off, but nothing can be further from the truth. Spices were incredibly expensive, and sauces were important not only to complement the taste of salted or bland meat or fish but to demonstrate how rich and important people were. A common saying was 'dear as pepper'. The quest for exotic spices drove the early explorers to cross the Atlantic, and later the Pacific, in search of a direct sea route to the Spice Islands, now known as the Maluku Islands, near Indonesia. During the reign of Elizabeth I, pepper was imported from India, cinnamon from Ceylon (now Sri Lanka), and nutmeg, mace and cloves from the Spice Islands. They were used to make spiced wines and to flavour fish, jam, soup and, particularly, meat dishes. The popularity of these spices saw European empires develop in India and Asia.

Another misconception until recent times was that the Tudors ate few vegetables, but this stems from the fact that few account books of the nobility feature their purchase. Instead they usually grew their own, and vegetables and fruit feature strongly in the recipes. However, people avoided uncooked vegetables and fruit, believing them to carry disease, and during a 1569 plague it became illegal to sell fresh fruit. Vegetables could only be eaten when they were in season as there was no way of storing food other than pickling. Typical vegetables were turnips, beans and cabbage. Fruit was cooked to make jam, preserves or fillings for pies. Common fruits were pears, apples, plums, damsons, cherries and strawberries. Some fruit was dried to use later in the year – dried apple rings, for example, were popular. If a family could afford luxuries, they might be able to buy oranges or lemons imported from Spain to make preserves and marmalades.

Ale or wine was served with meals – water was known to be dangerous and to carry diseases, even though the scientific proof was not to follow until the nineteenth century. Thus receipts (now recipes) call for 'faire water', i.e. spring or pure water, not well water which may be polluted. Rich puddings were served with spiced wine or whole spices (believed to aid digestion). Sugar became more popular, but was very expensive, leading to it being used only in the diet of the rich. On the tables of the nobility, there were figures moulded from jelly and pastry. At state banquets, these would be painted and gilded with sugar in the shape of ships, castles, churches, lions, crowns or birds, and known as *subtleties*, *conceites* or *extraordinaires*. It was discovered that fruit could be preserved in sugar, and jam and other conserves could be made with sugar. These uses of sugar had been known by the ancient Indians, Chinese and Arabs who had greater access to crystalline sugar. When sugar became more plentiful, but was still very expensive, a new passion arose. England copied Italy, and intricate spun-sugar sculpture (subtleties) became *de rigueur* for the tables of the rich. Majestic set pieces of sugar icing and *marchpane* (marzipan) were a part of the ostentatious display of wealth.

The popularity of sugar affected the history of the New World. By 1520 cane was growing in Mexico, and the Spanish explorer Cortes established the first North American sugar mill there in 1535. Cultivation spread to Peru, Brazil, Columbia, Venezuela and Puerto Rico by 1547, and by 1600 sugar production in the Americas had become the world's largest and most lucrative industry. The 'sugar islands' of the West Indies brought incredible wealth to England, and Elizabeth I displayed her wealth by putting a sugar bowl on her table and using sugar as an everyday snack and seasoning. This accounts for her black stumps for teeth.

Lacey Baldwin Smith's excellent biography of Catherine Howard tells us,

> In a period of three days, Elizabeth's court managed to consume 67 sheep, 34 pigs, 4 stags, 16 bucks (used to

make 176 meat pies), 1,200 chickens, 363 capons, 33 geese, 6 turkeys, 237 dozen pigeons, 2,500 eggs and 430 pounds of butter, plus a cartload and two horseloads of oysters. Such abundance was limited to State functions, but Henry VIII regularly spent over 1520 [pounds] a year on food for himself and his queen [around £860,000 in today's money], and the Duchess of Norfolk commonly sat down to a table set for twenty and served as her first course two boiled capons, a breast of mutton, a piece of beef, seven chevets [probably chewets, concoctions of meat or fish mixed with fruit or spices], a swan, a pig, a breast of veal, two roasted capons [fattened castrated cockerels], and a custard [open pie]. When Mr Henry Machyn, the undertaker, could polish off with the help of eight friends half a bushel of oysters, a quantity of onions, red ale, claret, and malmsey at eight in the morning, the extent of royal consumption, though still prodigious, no longer appears disproportionate to that of the rest of society. The usual royal fare consisted of such fattening delicacies as venison, mutton, carp, veal, swan, goose, stork, capon, conies, custard, fritters, and six gallons of beer and a sexter [pint] of wine to wash down what was only the first course. Then followed jellies, cream of almond, pheasant, hern [heron], bittern, partridge, quail, cocke gulles, kid, lamb, tarts, more fritters, eggs, butter, and finally fruit with powdered sugar. Not content with mere quantity, the eye as well as the stomach had to be satiated, and on special occasions dishes were transformed into a riot of colour and form, representing heraldic, historic and classical scenes. The rich man's table was loaded to overflowing and appetites matched the supply, but it must be remembered that waste was an economic necessity. Everybody from the household servant to the passing beggar was expected to make do with the leftovers.

The Catholic Church restricted the eating of meat on Wednesdays, Fridays and Saturdays, upon the vigils of certain saints' feast days and in Advent (the four weeks before Christmas) and Lent (the six weeks between

Carnival and Easter), so many non-meat dishes were made for these 'Lent Days'. In 1549, during Edward VI's reign, Fridays and Saturdays were re-established as non-meat days, along with Lent and some saints' days, and in 1563 Elizabeth I added Wednesdays. The latter law was to help the English fishing industry. Licences could be bought by the rich to overcome the restrictions. However, the impossibility of enforcing the laws meant that by the 1590s most wealthy houses were eating meat in Lent and on Fridays and Saturdays. Friday is still an obligatory 'fish day' for many, and in this way Christians were reminded of Jesus dying on the cross on Good Friday on a weekly basis. Other possible days of fasting for the devout were Wednesday, because of Judas' treason, and Saturday, to honour the Virgin Mary. Together with the weekly day, there was also an annual cycle of fasting days. Ember Days marked the beginning of the new season in December, March, June and September, and ember tarts and other dishes were made without meat. Taken as a whole, this means that meat was a prohibited food for a third to more than half of all the days in the year, which forced cooks to be adventurous in their use of vegetables, fruit and fish.

The eating of fish was allowed, possibly due to a belief that fish must be free of sin as they survived the Great Flood. The other explanation is that meat, especially red meat, would 'heat' the human body according to the theory of health 'humours'. A hot body was more susceptible to lust, and theologians saw a connection between the sins of the body (our 'meat') and the eating of meat. However fish brought a cold humour, and had a cooling effect on the human mind and body, and eating fish would lessen any sinful inclinations. For those near the coast, sea fish were easy to come by. Those inland had to rely on either freshwater fish, or salted or dried fish. The rich and the monasteries owned fishponds, to be assured of an ample supply of freshwater fish.

For Lent, the forty days of the withdrawal of Jesus into the wilderness, less the Sundays, there was an extra prohibition. At this time, not only meat, but also milk, butter, cheese and eggs were banned from the table. Almonds were very important, because these were the basis for almond milk, almond butter, and even almond cheese during Lent. All of these were used as replacement for forbidden dairy products. In February and March, at the end of winter, supplies of foods had run low, and what was left of the fruit and vegetables was old, except of course for some cabbages, turnips, onions and winter leeks. The staple diet at Lent consisted of bread (of poor quality for the poor), porridge or gruel made of grain (rye, spelt, wheat), dried peas, salted or dried vegetables, fish (fresh and preserved), onions, leeks, (old) apples and nuts, while the wealthy could afford dried dates, figs, raisin, currants and almonds.

Most recipe books give the order in which courses should be served, and the following example is from Thomas Dawson's *The Good Huswifes Jewell*, from 1596. Spellings vary in the original text for 'flesh daies' and 'fish daies', as reproduced here.

Here followeth the order of meat, how they must be Served at the Table, with their sauces for flesh daies at dinner.

The first course.
Potage or stewed broath, boyled meat or stewed meate, Chickins and Bacon, powdred [salted] Beefe, Pies, Goose, Pigge, Rosted Beefe, roasted Veale, Custard [an open pie of meat or vegetables].

The second course.
Roasted Lambe, Roasted Capons [castrated cocks], Roasted Conies [older rabbits], Chickins, Pehennes [peahens], Baked Venison, Tart.

The first course at Supper.
A Salet, A Pigges petitoe [trotter], Powdred Beefe slised, A Shoulder of Mutton or a Breast, Veale, Lambe, Custard [an open pie of vegetables, meat or fish].

The second course.
Capons roasted, Connies [rabbits] roasted, Chickins rosted, Pigions rosted, Larkes rosted, A pye of Pigions or Chickins, Baked Venison, Tart.

The service at Dinner.
A dosen of Quailes, A dishe of Larkes, Two pasties of red deare in a dish, Tarte,
Ginger bread, Fritters.

SERVICE FOR FISH DAIES

The first course.
Butter, a Sallet with hard Egges, potage of sand Eles, and Lamperns, Red Hearing [smoked herring – the strong smell gave a false scent to dogs], greene broyled [boiled greens] strewed upon, white Herring, Ling [*Molva molva*, similar to cod], Habardine [dried, salted cod], sauce Mustard, Salte Salmon minced, sauce Mustard, and Vergious [verjuice], and a little sugar, Powdred Gunger [salted conger eel?], Shadde [shad is similar to herring], Mackrell, Sauce vineger: Whyting: Sauce, with the Liver & Mustard. Playce: Sauce. Sorell, or Wine, and salt or mustard, or Vergious. Thorneback [ray]: sauce, Liver and mustard, Pepper and salt strowed upon, after it is brused. Fresh Cod: Sauce: greene sauce. Dace, Mullet, Eles upon soppes. Roche [roach] uppon soppes. Perch. Pike in Pikesauce. Trowte uppon soppes. Tench in Gelly or Geresill. Custard [an open pie of fish or vegetables].

The second course.
Flounders or Flokes [flukes, flatfish] pyke sauce. Fresh Salmon. Fresh Conger, Brette, Turbut, Halybut. Sauce vineger. Breame upon soppes. Carpe upon soppes. Soles or any other Fishes fried. Rosted Eele: Sauce the dripping. Rosted Lamperns [this is the river lamprey, *Lampetra fluviatilis*). Rosted Porpos. Fresh Sturgion. Galentine. Creuis [crayfish], Crab, Shrimps sauce vineger. Bakes Lampray [baked lampreys – this may be the sea lamprey, *Petromyzon marinus*, as it is spelt differently in the same menu], Tarte, figges, Apples, almonds blaunched, Cheese, Raysins, peares.

2. Tudor women carrying chickens and other produce from the market.
There were few shops, as such, for food provisions. There were local
general markets, but London had separate fish, meat and vegetable
markets, still operating today at Billingsgate, Smithfield and Covent
Garden respectively.

Meat Dishes

THE MEAT SEASONS

Thomas Dawson's *The good Huswifes Handmaide for the Kitchin*, 1594

'To knowe the due seasons for the use of al maner of meats throughout the yeare.

Brawn is best from holy Rood day til Lent, and at no other time commonlie used for service.

Bacon, Beefe and Mutton is good at all tymes, but the woorst tyme for Mutton is from Easter to Midsommer.

A fatte yoong Pig is never out of season.

A Goose is worst at Midsommer, & best in stubble tyme, but they be best of all when they be yoong green Geese.

Veale is all tymes good, but best in Januarie and Februarie. Kidde and yoong Lambe is best between Christmasse & Lent, & good from Easter to Whitsontide, but Kid is ever good.

Hennes be all times good, but best from Alhallowtyde to Lent. Fatte Capons [a large, castrated cockerel] be ever good.

Peacocks bee ever in season, but when they be yoong and of a good stature, they be as good as Feasants, & so be yoong Grouces. Sinets [probably snipe rather than cygnets] be best betweene Alhallowen day and Lent.

A Mallard is good after a frost, til Candlemas, so is a Teal and other wild foule that swimmeth.

A Woodcocke is best from October to Lent, and so be all other birdes, as Ousels, Thrushes and Robins, and such other. Herons, Curlewes, Crane, Bittour [bittern], Bussard [bustard], be at all times good, but best in Winter.

Feasant, Partridge and Raile, be ever good, but best when they bee taken with a Hawke, Quaile & Larks be ever good.

Connies [rabbits] be ever in season, but best from October to Lent.

A gelded Deare, whether he be fallow or red, is ever good. A Pollard [a deer that has shed its antlers] is speciallie good in May, at Midsommer he is a Bucke, and verie good till Holy Rood day before Michaelmas, so likewise is a Stagge, but he is principal in Maie. A barren Doe is best in Winter. A Pricket [juvenile fallow deer buck] and a Sorell syster [a sorell fallow buck is over three years old, and presumably this is a similar doe] is ever in season.

Chickens bee ever good: and so be yoong Pigeons.'

FARTS OF PORTINGALE – PORTUGUESE MERCHANT FARTS

Thomas Dawson's *The good Huswifes Handmaide for the Kitchin*, 1594

'How to make Farts of Portingale. Take a piece of a leg of Mutton, mince it small and season it with cloves, mace, pepper, salt and dates minced with currants. Then roll it into round rolls, and so into little balls. Boil them in a little beef broth and so serve them forth.'

MEAT PEARS OR MEAT BALLS

Thomas Dawson's *The Second part of The Good Huswifes Jewell*, 1597

'To make Peares to be boild in meate. Take a piece of a leg of mutton or raw veal, being mixed with a little sheep suet, and half a manchet [fine white loaf] grated fine, adding four raw eggs yolks. Then take a little thyme & parsley chopped small, and a few gooseberries or barberries, or whole green grapes. Put all these together, being seasoned with salt, saffron and cloves, beaten and wrought altogether. Then make rolls or balls similar to a pear. When you have so done, take the stalk of the sage, and put it into the ends of your pears or balls [to make it appear like a fruit]. Then take the fresh beef, mutton or veal broth, put into an earthen pot, and add the pears or balls in the same broth with salt, cloves, mace and saffron. When you are ready to serve, put two or three yolks of eggs into the broth. Let them boil no more after that, but serve it upon sop [pieces of bread or toast]. You may make balls after the same manner.'

PRETEND FOREIGN STEWE

A Proper New Booke of Cookery, 1545 and 1575

'To make a stewe after the guyse of beyond the Sea. Take a pottle [4 pints] of fair [spring] water, and add as much wine. Place in it a breast of mutton chopped into pieces, and then set it on the fire. Remove scum, and add a dishful of sliced onions, with a quantity of cinnamon, ginger, cloves, mace and salt, and stew them all together, and then serve them with sops.'

[Wine was much cheaper proportionately than today].

PYGGE Y-FARSYD – STUFFED PIGLET, GOAT OR SHEEP

A Noble Boke off Cookry ffor a Prynce Houssolde, Holkham MSS 674, 1480/1500

'Pygge y-farsyd. Take raw eggs, and draw them through a strainer. Then grate fair bread. Take saffron, salt, pepper powder and mutton suet, and meld all together in a faire boil [simmer to reduce]. Then broach [spit roast] thine pig; then farce [stuff] him [with the above stuffing], and sew the hole, and let him roast; and then serve forth.'

[Mutton suet is the charmless 'swet of a schepe' in the original recipe.]

3. Elizabeth I is offered a knife to make the first cut in butchering the deer caught by the hunt. Venison was very popular among the nobility in Tudor times, and all the Tudor monarchs enjoyed hunting.

MINST PYES

The Good Hous-wiues Treasurie, 1588

'To make minst Pyes. Take your veal or mutton and parboil it a little, then set it to cool. When it is cold, take 3 pounds of suet to a leg of mutton, or 4 pounds to a fillet of veal [as it is less fatty], and then mince them small. You can mix them together if you wish. Then to season add half an ounce of nutmeg, half an ounce of cloves and mace, half an ounce of cinnamon, a little pepper, and as much salt as you think will season them, either to the mutton or to the veal. Take 8 yolks of eggs when they are hard, half a pint of rosewater full measure, half a pound of sugar, and strain the yolks with the rosewater and sugar and mingle it with your meat. If you have any oranges or lemons you must take 2 of them, and take the peels very thin and mince them very small. Put the minced peels in a pound of currants, 6 dates, and half a pound of prunes. Lay the currants and dates upon the top of your meat. You must take two or three Pomewaters [extinct apples] or wardens [hard pears] and mince with your meat, you can use less if you wish. If you will make good [pie] crust, put in 3 or 4 yolks of eggs, a little rosewater, & a good deal of sugar.' [This recipe is rare in that it gives quantities of ingredients.]

ALLOES OF BEEF – BEEF OLIVES

Gentyll Manly Cokere, MS Pepys 1047, *c.* 1490

'To make Alloes of beef. Take lean beef and cut into thin pieces and lay on a board. Then take mutton or beef suet, and herbs and onions hacked small together. Then strew your slices of beef with powder of pepper and a little salt, and strew on your suet and herbs. And roll them up therein, put them on a spit [or skewer] and roast them and serve them up hot.'

ALOES OF VEAL OR MUTTON – MOCK LARKS

Thomas Dawson's *The Second part of The Good Huswifes Jewell*, 1597

'To bake aloes of Veal or Mutton. Make your aloes ready to bake in all points as you boil them, laying barberries, gooseberries or green grapes upon them in the pastry, or small raisins, and put in your pie a dish of butter. So set it in the oven, and when it is baked, then put in a little verjuice* [wine vinegar], and so seethe it in an oven again a while, and so serve it forth.'

*Verjuice can be the unripe juice of grapes or apples.

ALOES – VEAL OR MUTTON COOKED TO RESEMBLE LARKS

Thomas Dawson's *The Good Huswifes Jewell*, 1596

'To make Aloes. Take a leg of veal or mutton, and slice thinly, and lay in a platter, and cast on salt. Put thereon the yolks of 10 eggs, and a great assortment of small raisons and dates finely minced. Then take vinegar, a little saffron, cloves, mace and a little pepper, and mingle together. Pour it all about, and then work it all together, and when it is thoroughly seasoned, put it on a spit. Set platters underneath it [to catch the fat], and baste it with butter, and then make a sauce with vinegar, ginger and sugar [probably mixing with the fat in the platters]. Lay the aloes upon it and so serve it.'

PYE OF ALOES – MOCK LARK PIE

A Proper New Booke of Cookery, 1545 and 1575

'To make a pye of Aloes. Take a leg of mutton, and cut it in thin slices, and for stuffing take parsley, thyme and savoury, and chop them small. Then temper among them

3 or 4 yolks of hard-boiled eggs chopped small with small raisins, dates, mace and a little salt. Then lay all these in the mutton steaks, and then roll them together. This done, make your pie, and lay all these therein. Then season them with a little sugar, cinnamon, saffron and salt. Then cast upon them the yolks of 3 or 4 hard-boiled eggs, with cut dates and small raisins. Close your pie, and bake. Then for a syrup take toasted bread and a little claret wine, and strain them thinly together. Add to it a little sugar, cinnamon and ginger, and put it into your pie, and then serve it forth.'

VEAL BAKE MEATE – VEAL OLIVES
Thomas Dawson's *The Good Huswifes Jewell*, 1596

'Another bake meate. Take a leg of veal, and cut it in slices, and beat it with the back of a knife. Then take thyme, marjoram, pennyroyal, savoury, parsley and one onion, and chop them altogether very small. Then break in some egg whites and mix all, and put in your herbs and season with pepper, nutmeg, salt and a little sugar. Then stir them altogether, and then form into shapes like beef olives. Cast a few currants, dates and butter amongst them.'

STEWED VEAL
Thomas Dawson's *The Second part of The Good Huswifes Jewell*, 1597

'To stewe veal. Take a knuckle of veal, then set it on the fire in a little fresh water, and let it seethe a good while. Then take plenty of onions and chop them into your broth, and when it is well cooked, put in verjuice, butter, salt and saffron, and when it is enough add a little sugar, and then it will be good.'

VEALE OR MUTTON PYES
A. W.'s *A Book of Cookrye*, 1584 and 1591
'For fine Pyes of Veale or Mutton. Parboil your meat and shred it fine, and shred your suet by itself. When your suet is finely shred, add it to your mutton or veal and mince them together. Add half a dozen yolks of hard-boiled eggs and small currants and dates, both finely minced. Season it with cloves and mace, cinnamon and ginger, a very little pepper, a handful of caraway, sugar, verjuice and some salt. Put it into your pastry, making Chewets or Trunk pyes [small or large pies].'

ROAST VEAL FILLET
The Good Hous-wiues Treasurie, 1588
'How to roste the Fillet of a legge of Veale. Take the fat of the kidney. Cut it in pieces as big as one's finger. Then take pepper, salt and nutmeg, and cover it with that and the fat together, and let it be very well roasted. Then make venison sauce to add to it with vinegar, grated bread, cinnamon, sugar, a little pepper and two or three whole cloves.'

VEAL TOASTS (1)
Thomas Dawson's *The Second part of The Good Huswifes Jewell*, 1597
'To make Toasts. Take the kidney of veal and chop it small. Then set it on a chafingdish of charcoal, and take two yolks of eggs, currants, cinnamon, ginger, cloves, mace and sugar. Let them boil together a good while, and add a little butter to the kidney.'
[A chafing dish was a grating on a brazier, a little like today's barbecue].

TOASTS OF VEAL (2)
Thomas Dawson's *The good Huswifes Handmaide for the Kitchin*, 1594
'To make toasts of Veal. Take the kidneys, chop them very small, then add 4 or 5 yolks of eggs, 3 spoonfuls of sugar, a little cinnamon and ginger, and a spoonful of currants, clean washed and picked. Chop them all together, then make sops of stale white bread, and lay your stuff upon them. Take a frying pan and a dish of sweet [unsalted] butter in it, and melt it. Then put in your toasts and fry them upon a soft fire. Then lay them in a dish, and cast sugar on them. Your fire must be very soft, or else they will burn.'

A RARE CONCEIT, WITH VEAL BAKED
Thomas Dawson's *The good Huswifes Handmaide for the Kitchin*, 1594
'To make a rare Conceit, with Veal baked. Take veal and cut it in pieces, and seethe it in fair water. Then take parsley, sage, hyssop and savoury, and shred them small. Put them in the pot when it boils. Take powder of pepper, canel [canella, an inferior form of cinnamon], mace, saffron and salt, and let all these boil together till it be enough. Then remove the veal from the broth, and let the broth cool. When it is cold, take the yolks of eggs with the whites, and strain them, and put them into the broth, so many till the broth be stiff enough. Then make fair coffins [pastry cases], and couch 3 or 4 pieces of the veal in one coffin. Take minced dates and prunes, powder of pepper, ginger and verjuice, and put it into the broth. Then put the liquor in the coffins, as you do with a custard [open pie], and bake it till cooked, and so serve it forth.'

SWEET PIES OF VEAL

Thomas Dawson's *The good Huswifes Handmaide for the Kitchin*, 1594

'To make sweet pies of Veal. Take veal and parboil it very tender, then chop it small, then take twice as much beef suet, and chop it small. Then mince both together. Then add currants and minced dates, then season your veal after this manner. Take pepper, salt, saffron, cloves, mace, cinnamon, ginger and sugar, and season your meat with each of these, mixing them altogether. Then take fine flour, butter, eggs and saffron, & make your pastry withall as fine as you can, and make your pie with it. And when it is made, fill it with your stuffs. Then put upon your pie, prunes, currants, dates, a little sugar, and hard-boiled yolks of eggs. Then cover your pie and set it on a paper, and set it in the oven, and let it bake. If it be scorched above lay a double paper on it [only the very rich had ovens].'

CHEWITES OF VEAL

Thomas Dawson's *The good Huswifes Handmaide for the Kitchin*, 1594

'To make Chewites of Veal. Take a leg of veal and parboil it, then mince it with beef suet. Take almost as much of your suet as of your veal, and take a good quantity of ginger, & a little saffron to colour it. Take half a goblet of white wine, and two or three good handfuls of grapes, and put them all together with salt, and so put them in coffins [pastry containers], and let them boil a quarter of an hour.'

BOILED MEATS FOR SUPPER

Thomas Dawson's *The Good Huswifes Jewell*, 1596

'To boyle meates for supper. Take veal and put it into a posnet [a small basin] with carrot roots cut in long pieces, then boil it and add thereto a handful of prunes and crumbs of bread. Then season it with pepper, salt and vinegar.'

BALLES OF ITALIE – VEAL BALLS IN BEEF OR MUTTON BROTH

Thomas Dawson's *The good Huswifes Handmaide for the Kitchin*, 1594

'To make balles of Italie. Take a piece of a leg of veal, parboil it, then pare away all the skin and sinews and chop the veal very small. Add a little salt and pepper, 2 yolks of Eggs hard roasted, and 7 yolks raw. Temper all these with your veal, then make balls thereof as big as walnuts. Boil them in beef broth, or mutton broth, as you did the other before rehearsed, and put into your broth 10 beaten cloves, a race [sprig or root] of ginger, a little verjuice, and 4 or 5 lumps of whole marrow. Let them stew the space of an hour. Then serve them upon [bread] sops, 8 or 9 in a dish, and betwixt the balls you must lay the lumps of marrow.'

VAUTES – STUFFED PANCAKES

A Proper New Booke of Cookery, 1545 and 1575

'To make Vautes. Take the kidney of veal, and parbol it till it be tender, then take and chop it small with the yolks of 3 or 4 eggs. Then season it with dates cut small, small raisins, ginger, sugar, cinnamon, saffron and a little salt. For the pastry to lay it in, take 12 eggs, both the whites and the yolks, and beat them well altogether. Then take butter and put into a frying pan and fry them as thin as a pancake, then lay your filling therein. And so fry them together in a pan, and cast sugar and ginger upon it, and so serve it forth.'

STOCKFRITURES
A Proper New Booke of Cookery, 1545 and 1575
'To make stockfritures. Take the same stuffe that you take to a vaut [see vaute recipe above], and that same paste ye take for Pescods [recipe below], and ye may fry them or else bake them.'

PESCODS – MARROW AFTER THE MANNER OF PEAPODS (1)
John Partridge's *The Treasurie of commodious Conceits*, 1573
'To make Pescods of Marow. First slice your marrow in length, and roll your pastry as thin as a paper leaf. Then take and lay small raisins, cinnamon and a little ginger and sugar about the marrow, fashion them up like peapods, and fry them in butter. Cast upon them cinnamon and sugar, and serve them.'

MARROW AFTER THE MANNER OF PEAPODS (2)
A Proper New Booke of Cookery, 1545 and 1575
'To make Pescoddes. Take marrow bones, and pull the marrow out of them, and cut into two parts. Then season with sugar, cinnamon, ginger and a little salt, and make your pastry as fine as you can, and as short and thin as you can. Then fry them in sweet suet, and cast upon them a little cinnamon and ginger, and so serve them at the table.'

STEW OF FLESH – BEEF AND CHICKEN STEW
Gentyll Manly Cokere, MS Pepys 1047, *c.* 1490
'To make a stew of flesh. If your pot is 4 gallons, add in a quart [2 pints] of wine. Add fair beef of the foreloin

or of the hind loin and mince it, and add good capons [castrated cockerels or large chickens]. Take pepper, good powder of canell, ginger, raisins of Corance [Corinth raisins are currants], cloves, mace, saffron & saunders [sandalwood]. Add onions, parsley, sage, rosemary, thyme, hyssop, savory, clarified honey*, and a quantity [large amount] of bruised almonds. Bring to the boil, but you need to have a charcoal fire for burning, and not too great a fire but a small good for boiling fire. And boil well in the stewing. And take care your pot is well covered, so the heat does not escape. And thus stew all manner of meat.'

*Supplies of honey, the regular sweetener, declined drastically because of the Dissolution of the Monasteries. Monks and nuns were the major honey producers, because honey was a by-product of beeswax production, used for making expensive candles (the poor used tallow, from animal fats). Increasing availability of sugar replaced it in the upper classes.

SEWES – RUMP OF BEEF STEWED WITH CABBAGE AND BIRDS

A Proper New Booke of Cookery, 1545 and 1575

'To make Sewes. Take a rump of beef and let it boil an hour or two. Then add a great quantity of coleworts [any *brassica* such as cabbage and kale], and let them boil together for three hours. Then add to them a couple of stock doves or teal, pheasant, partridge, or such other wildfowl, and let them boil all together. Then season them with salt, and serve them forth.'

PRESERVED BEEF

Thomas Dawson's *The Good Huswifes Jewell*, 1596

'To bake a Fillet of beefe to keepe colde. Mince it very small, and seethe it with pepper and salt, and make it up together accordingly. Put it in your pie, and lard it very thick.'

[This is to preserve a pie in a cold larder, for later consumption or for travel].

TO STUE BEEFE

Thomas Dawson's *The good Huswifes Handmaide for the Kitchin*, 1594

'To stue Beefe. Take beef and smite it in pieces, and wash it in fair water. Strain that water and put it in the pot with the beef, and boil them together. Then take pepper, cloves, mace, onions, parsley and sage. Cast into the pot let it boil together. Then make liquor with bread and thicken it. And so let it seethe a good while after that to thicken it. Then put in saffron, salt and vinegar, and so serve it forth.'

BULLY BEEF

Traditional

Meat such as pork and beef was packed into barrels and covered with salt to preserve it at sea. Salt beef was usually boiled to make it edible, and the French *boeuf bouillé* became 'bully beef'. Sometimes the meat was too tough to eat, and the sailors made snuffboxes or ornaments out of it to pass the time. It was in the interest of the ship's cook to boil meat extremely well, as all the fat and grease could be used by the cook to make tallow or candles, a perk of the job.

VAUNT

Thomas Dawson's *The good Huswifes Handmaide for the Kitchin*, 1594

'To make a Vaunt. Take marrow of beef, as much as you can hold in both your hands, and cut it as big as great dice. Then take 10 dates, and cut them as big as small dice. Then take 30 prunes and cut the fruit from the stones. Then take half a handful of currants, wash them and pick them, then put your marrow in a clean platter, and your dates, prunes, and currants. Then take 10 yolks of eggs, and put into your mixture afore rehearsed. Then take a quartern [¼ pint] of sugar, and more, and beat it small and add to your marrow. Then take two spoonfuls of cinnamon, and a spoonful of sugar, and add them to your mixture, and mingle them all together. Then take 8 yolks of eggs, and 4 spoonfuls of rosewater, strain them, and add a little sugar to it. Then take a fair frying pan, and put a little piece of butter in it, as much as a walnut, and set it upon a good fire, and when it looks almost black, put it out of your pan.

As fast as you can, put half of the yolks of the eggs into the middle of your pan, and let it run all the breadth of your pan, and fry it fair and yellow. When it is fried put it in a fair dish, and put your mixture therein, and spread it all over the bottom of the dish. Then make another vaunt even as you made the other, and set it upon a fair board and cut it in fair slices, of the breadth of your little finger, as long as your vaunt is. Then lay it upon your mixture after the fashion of a lattice window, and then cut off the ends of them, as much as lies without the inward compass of the dish. Then set the dish within the oven or in a baking pan, and let it bake at leisure, and when it is baked enough the marrow will come fair out of the vaunt, unto the brim of the dish. Then draw it out, and cast thereon a little sugar, and so you may serve it.'

BAKED CALVES FEET AFTER THE FRENCH FASHION

Thomas Dawson's *The good Huswifes Handmaide for the Kitchin*, 1594

'To bake Calves feet after the French fashion. Take the feet, pull off the hair, make them clean, and boil them a little till they are somewhat tender. Then make your pastry, and season your calves' feet with pepper, salt and cinnamon, and put them in your pastry, with a quantity of sweet [unsalted] butter, parsley and onions. Close it up, and set into the oven until half baked. Then take them forth, and open the crown, and put in more butter & some vinegar, so let them stand in the oven till they are thoroughly baked.'

TRIPES ON BREAD

A Proper New Booke of Cookery, 1545 and 1575

'To stewe Trypes. Take a pint of claret wine, and set it upon the fire and cut your tripes in small pieces. Thereto add in a good quantity of cinnamon and ginger, and also a sliced onion or two. And so let them boil half an hour, & then serve them upon sops.'

SKILLYGOLEE, SKILLY

Tudor tradition

When salt meat was boiled to make it edible, the water was then mixed with oatmeal to make a savoury broth or thick soup. It was served to naval prisoners, and prisoners of war kept in hulks. Skillygolee, or skillygallee, later became an oatmeal drink sweetened with sugar (in place of cocoa) for seamen during the Napoleonic Wars (1803–1815).

MARY BONE AND CARROT BROTH

Thomas Dawson's *The Second part of The Good Huswifes Jewell*, 1597

'To boyle mary bones for for dinner. First put your marrow bones into a fair pot of water, and let them boil till they are half cooked. Then take out all your broth save as much as will cover your marrow bones. Then put in 8 or 9 carrots, and see they are well scraped and washed, and cut an inch long or a little less. Add a handful of parsley and hyssop chopped small, and season it with salt, pepper and saffron. You may boil chines and racks [backbones and ribs] of veal in all points as this is.'

[This author's deceased aunt used to use an old marrow spoon to scoop out marrow from bones – it was her favourite food, and wholesome, but now seems to be avoided. We see Georgian silver marrow scoops in antique shops, an elegant solution to a problem of getting marrow out of meat bones without abandoning one's table manners. Forks were not used in Tudor times, and when they appeared, they did not help in taking the savoury jelly out of the marrowbones. *Youths Behaviour*, an etiquette book translated from French by Francis Hawkins in 1646, told diners to stop handling and 'mouthing' bones altogether, but he would allow you to use one hand for meat bones as long as there was no banging, cracking, biting, gnawing, sucking or slurping. Hawkins tells us to 'get the marrow out neatly and decently – with a knife. Suck no bones ... Take them not with two hands ... Gnaw them not ... Knock no bones upon thy bread, or trencher, to get out the marrow of them, but get out the marrow with a knife ... To speake better ... it is not fit to handle bones, and much lesse to mouth them. Make not use of a knife to breake bones... also breake them not with thy teeth, or other thing, but let them alone.' Today at last we are seeing diet and health books extolling the benefits of bone broths.]

PETTIE SERVICES – EGG AND MARROW PIE

Thomas Dawson's *The good Huswifes Handmaide for the Kitchin*, 1594

'Pettie services. Take fair flour, saffron & sugar, and make thereof pastry. Make thereof coffins, and take the yolks of eggs, see the yolks be all whole. Then lay 3 or 4 eggs in the coffin, and two or three pieces of marrow. Then take powder of ginger, sugar and currants, and roll the marrow in them, and put all in the pie. Cover it, or bake it in a pan.'

SMALL MARROW PIES

Thomas Dawson's *The Second part of The Good Huswifes Jewell*, 1597

'For small pies. Take the marrow out of the marybone's hole, and cut it in the bigness of a bean. Season your marrow with ginger, sugar and cinnamon, then put them in fine pastry. Fry them in a frying pan with the skimming of fresh beef broth. Or else you may bake them in your oven a little, while taking heed they do not burn. And when you do serve them in a fair dish, cast blaunch pouder [spelt many ways, a spice mixture of sugar, ginger and nutmeg] upon them.'

4. Woodcut of an English wild boar from the title page of a book published in London in 1593. Boar was only eaten by nobles.

A PODYNG OF A NOX – BEEF OR LAMB BLOOD SAUSAGES

Gentyll Manly Cokere, MS Pepys 1047, *c.* 1490

'To make A podyng of A nox or of A shepe. Take the blood and swing it with thy hand and cast away the lumps that come. Then take suet of the same and mince it small and put into the blood. Also put in plenty of oats and fill up your ropeys [intestines which act as sausage casings] with the same and seethe them, and after broil them when they be cold. And serve them forth.'

LONGLIFE WILDE BOAR PASTIES

Thomas Dawson's *The good Huswifes Handmaide for the Kitchin*, 1594

'To bake a wilde Boare. Take 3 parts of water, and the 4th part of white wine, and put thereto salt, as much as shall season it. Let the boar boil until almost cooked. Then take it out of the broth, and let it lie till it is thoroughly cold. Then lard it, and lay it in coarse pastry, in pasties, and then season it with pepper, salt and ginger. Put in twice so much ginger as pepper. And when it is half baked, fill your pasties with white wine, and shake each pasty. And then put the pasties into the oven again, till cooked. Then let them stand 5 or 6 days, or ever that you eat of them, and that time it will be very good meat.'

HOG SAUSAGES

The Good Hous-wiues Treasurie, 1588

'How to make Sausages. Take the fillets of a hog, and half as much of the suet of the hog, and chop them both very small. Then take grated bread, 2 or 3 yolks of eggs, a spoonful of groce* pepper, and as much salt. Temper with a little cream, and so put them into the skins and broil them on a grid-iron.'

*Spelt grose, grosse, gross, etc.; it means grocer's pepper, or large pepper, peppercorns rather than powdered or ground pepper.

PORK FILLETS IN GALLENTINE SAUCE
Thomas Dawson's *The good Huswifes Handmaide for the Kitchin*, 1594

'To make fillets Gallentine. Take fair pork, and take off the skin and roast it till half cooked. Then take it off the spit, and smite it in fair pieces, and cast it in a fair pot. Then cut onions, but not too small, and fry them in fair suet, and put them into the pork. Then take the broth of beef or mutton, and add thereto, and set them on the fire. Add thereto powder of pepper, saffron, cloves and mace, and let them boil well together. Then take fair bread and vinegar, & steep the bread with some of the same broth, and strain it. Add some blood, or else saunders [sandalwood, red food colouring], and colour it with that, and let all boil together, then cast in a little saffron and salt, and then you may serve it.'

FOR TO BAKE A PIGGE
Thomas Dawson's *The good Huswifes Handmaide for the Kitchin*, 1594

'For to bake a Pigge. Flay your pig, and take out all that is within his belly clean, and wash him well, and after parboil him. Then season it with pepper, salt, nutmeg, mace and cloves, and so lay it with good store of butter in the pastry. Then set it in the oven till it be baked enough.'

ROAST PIGGE

Thomas Dawson's *The Second part of The Good Huswifes Jewell*, 1597

'To roast a Pigge. Take your pig and draw it, and wash it clean, and take the liver. Parboil it and strain it with a little cream, and yolks of eggs. Add thereto grated bread, marrow, small raisins, nutmegs in powder, mace, sugar and salt. Stir all these together, and put into the pig's belly, and sow the pig. Then put in on a spit with the hair on, & when it is half cooked, pull off the skin, and take heed you take not off the fat. Then baste it, and when it is enough, then crumb it with white bread, sugar, cinnamon and ginger, and let it be somewhat brown.'

TO BAKE A PIG LIKE A FAWNE OR A KID

Thomas Dawson's *The good Huswifes Handmaide for the Kitchin*, 1594

'To bake a Pig like a Fawne. Take him when he is in the hair, and flay him, then season with pepper & salt, cloves and mace. Then take claret wine, verjuice, rosewater, sugar, cinnamon and ginger, and boil them all together. Then lay your pig flat like a fawn or a kid, and put your syrup unto it, with a little sweet butter, and so bake it leisurely.'

TO SOWCE A PIGGE – PORK SAUCE

Thomas Dawson's *The good Huswifes Handmaide for the Kitchin*, 1594

'To sowce a Pigge. You must take white wine, & a little sweet broth, and half a score of nutmegs cut in quarters. Then take sweet marjoram, rosemary, bay and thyme and let them boil all together. Scum [skim] them very clean.

When boiled, put them in an earthen pan, and the syrup also. And when you serve them, a quarter in a dish, and place the bays and nutmegs on the top.'

PYES OF PAIRIS – PARISIAN PORK AND VEAL COFFINS
A Noble Boke off Cookry ffor a Prynce Houssolde, Holkham MSS 674, 1480/1500

'To mak pyes of pairis. Take and smite fair butts of pork and butts of veal and put together in a pot with fresh broth. Add a quantity of wine and boil it till cooked then put it into a treen [wooden] vessel. Add raw yolks of eggs, powder of ginger, sugar, salt, minced dates and currants and make a good thin pastry and make coffins. Put the mix in, bake well and serve.'

TO BOIL TRIPE, PIGS TROTTERS OR CATTLE FEET
Thomas Dawson's *The good Huswifes Handmaide for the Kitchin,* 1594

'To boil tripes, pigs petietots or Neates feet. Take your cattle feet, tripes, or trotters, and cut them in small pieces, and boil them with butter, cinnamon, currants, and a little vinegar, and serve them upon sops.'

BASTARDISED PIGS' TROTTERS
Thomas Dawson's *The Good Huswifes Jewell,* 1596

'To boile pigges feete and petitoes. Take and boil them in a pint of verjuice & bastard [a sweet Spanish wine like Muscadel]. Take 4 dates minced with a few small raisons. Then take a little thyme and chop it small and season it with a little cinnamon and ginger and a quantity of verjuice.'

GAMMON PIE
Thomas Dawson's *The Good Huswifes Jewell*, 1596
'To bake a Gammon of Bacon. Take a Gammon of Bacon, water it 6 days and parboil till half-cooked. Lay it in a press then take the sword of it and stuff it with cloves. Season with pepper and saffron, and close up in a standing pie, bake and serve.'

BAKED HERB-STUFFED GAMMON PIE
Thomas Dawson's *The good Huswifes Handmaide for the Kitchin*, 1594
'For to bake a Gammon of Bacon. Boil your gammon of bacon. When it has boiled, stuff it with parsley, sage and yolks of hard-boiled eggs. Let it boil again. Season it with pepper, cloves and mace, and stick whole cloves fast in it. Then lay it so in your pastry with salted butter, and so bake it.'

COLD GAMMON
Thomas Dawson's *The Good Huswifes Jewell*, 1596
'To bake a Gammon of bacon to keepe colde. You must first boil it a quarter of an hour before you stuff it, and stuff it with sweet herbs, and hard eggs chopped together, or parsley.'

FARSED BANQUET CABBADGE – MEAT-STUFFED CABBAGE
Thomas Dawson's *The Second part of The Good Huswifes Jewell*, 1597
'To farse a cabbadge for a banquet dish. Take little round cabbage, cutting off the stalks, and then make a round hole

in your cabbage, as much as will receive your farsing meat [stuffing]. Take heed you break not the brims thereof with your knife, for the hole must be round and deep. Then take the kidney of mutton or more, and chop it not small. Then boil 6 eggs hard. Chop small the yolks of them, & also take raw eggs and a manchet [white loaf] grated fine. Then take a handful of prunes, so many great raisins, seasoning all these with salt, pepper, cloves and mace, working all these together, and so stuff your cabbage. But if you have sawsedge [sausage] you may put it among your meat at the putting in of your stuff, but you must leave out both the ends of your sausage at the mouth of the cabbage when you shall serve it out. In boiling it must be within the cabbage, and the cabbage must be stopped close with a cover in the time of boiling, and bound fast roundabout [to prevent] breaking. The cabbage must be cooked in a deep pot with fresh beef or mutton broth, and no more they will lie unto the top of the cabbage. When it is enough cooked take away the third [thread holding it], and so set it in a platter, opening the head & laying out the sausage ends, and so serve it forth.'

[In the original recipe alone, sausage is spelt three ways – sawsedge, sawsage and sawsadge. There is an Elizabethan recipe for sawsedge, written in 1602, following.]

POLONIAN SAWSEDGE – POLISH SAUSAGE
Sir Hugh Plat's *Delightes for Ladies*, 1602

'To make a Polonian sawsedge. Take the fillets of a hog, chop them very small, with a handful of red [purple] sage. Season it hot with ginger and pepper, and then put it into a great sheep's gut, then let it lie 3 nights in brine. Then boil it and hang it up in a chimney where fire is usually kept, and these sausages will last one whole year. They are good for salads, or to garnish boiled meats, or to make one relish a cup of wine.'

[This is possibly Plat's cook's attempt at recreating Polish *krajana* or *siekana kielbasa*. The sausages are stuffed, then cured in brine, blanched and hung up in a chimney. The recipe states they will keep for a year and will engender a mighty thirst. Ned Ward's *London Spy* (1698–99) described the Spaniards as being recognised by their smell, 'for they Stink as Strong of Garlick as a Polonian Sausage', displaying the true Englishman's active and lasting distaste for 'Johnny Foreigner'.]

MEAT AND VINEGAR PIE
Thomas Dawson's *The Good Huswifes Jewell*, 1596

'To make a pie. First parboil your flesh and press it. When it is pressed, season it with pepper and salt while it is hot. Then lard it. Make your pastry from rye flour. It must bee very thick, or else it will not hold. [Pastry cases were used instead of dishes to hold food when cooking, and often became black and almost inedible.] When it is seasoned and larded lay it in your pie, then cast a good deal of cloves and mace, beaten small, on it before you close it. Throw upon that a good deal of butter, and so close it up. You must leave a hole in the top of the lid, & when it has stood 2 hours in the oven, you must fill it as full of vinegar as you can, and then stop the hole as close as you can with pastry. [Vinegar helped preserve the contents of sealed pies.] Then set it into the oven again. Your oven must be very hot at the first, so that your pies will keep a great while. The longer you keep them, the better they will be. When they are taken out of the oven and almost cold, you must shake them between your hands, and set them with the bottom upward. When you set them into the oven, be well aware that one pie touch not another by more than ones hand's breadth. Remember also to let them stand in the oven after the vinegar is in, for 2 hours and more.'

[An almost identical recipe is given by Dawson in *The good Huswifes Handmaide for the Kitchin* of 1594, under the heading 'To make a pie to keep long'.]

BOILED MEATS FOR DINNER

Thomas Dawson's *The Good Huswifes Jewell*, 1596

'To make boyled meates for dinner. Take the ribs of a neck of mutton, and stuff it with marjoram, savoury, thyme, parsley, chopped small currants, with the yolks of two eggs, pepper & salt. Then put it into a posnet [small basin, porringer] with fair water, or else with the liquor of some meat, with vinegar, pepper, salt and a little butter, and so serve.'

BOILED MUTTON SUPPER

Thomas Dawson's *The Second part of The Good Huswifes Jewell*, 1597

'Mutton boild for supper. First set your mutton on the fire, & trim it clean. Then take out all the broth, saving so much as will cover it. Then take and put thereto 10 or 12 onions pilled [peeled], cut into quarters, with a handful of parsley chopped fine, putting it with the mutton. And so let them boil, seasoning it with pepper, salt and saffron, with two or three spoonfuls of vinegar.'

STEWED MUTTON STEAKS (1)

A Proper New Booke of Cookery, 1545 and 1575

'To stew steekes of Mutton. Take a leg of mutton, and cut it in small slices, and put it in a chafer, and put thereto a pottle [4 pints] of ale. Scum [skim derivates from scum] it clean, then put thereto 7 or 8 onions thinly sliced. After they have boiled one hour, add a dish of sweet [unsalted] butter, and so let them boil till they be tender, and then put thereto a little pepper and salt.'

[Ale was drunk by everyone, and nearly all wives made it as it was safer than water. 'Small beer' was weak ale brewed for invalids and children.]

STEWED MUTTON STEAKES (2)

Thomas Dawson's *The good Huswifes Handmaide for the Kitchin*, 1594

'To make stewed steakes. Take the breast of mutton, cut it in pieces and wash it clean. Then put it in a fair pot and fill your pot with ale, or half wine and half water. Make it seethe and scum it clean. Then put into your pot a faggot of thyme, rosemary and parsley [like a *bouquet garni*], and three or four onions cut around. Take a little parsley picked very small, and let them boil altogether. Then take prunes, small raisins and great dates, and let them boil altogether. Then season your pot with these spices. Take salt and a little saffron, cloves, mace, cinnamon, ginger, & a little sugar. Take a quantity of these spices, and put them into your pot, & let them stew all together, and when they are tender, add a little verjuice. Let them stew again, then lay sops of a manchet [pieces of white bread] under them in a platter, [but] at the first you must put a good deal of marrow in it.'

STEWED MUTTON STEAKES (3)

Thomas Dawson's *The Good Huswifes Jewell*, 1596

'To make stewed Steakes. Take a piece of mutton, and cut it in pieces, and wash it very clean, and put it into a faire pot with ale, or with half wine. Then make it boil, and scum it clean, and put into your pot a faggot of rosemary and thyme. Then take some parsley picked fine, and some onions cut round, and let them all boil together, then take prunes, raisons, dated and currants and let it boil all together, and season it with cinnamon, ginger, nutmegs, 2 or 3 Cloves, and salt. Serve it on sops, and garnish it with fruit.'

[The Tudors were much more adventurous with mixing many fruits, such as lemon, orange, apple, pear, prune, damson, date, currant, raisin, sultana, redcurrant, blackcurrant, quince, blackberry, gooseberry, grape, barberry, hazelnuts, walnuts etc., with meats and fish. Honey was often used in dishes, as sugar was still incredibly expensive. Today we only regularly see pineapple with gammon.]

MUTTON STEAK BROTH

Thomas Dawson's *The Second part of The Good Huswifes Jewell*, 1597

'To stew Steakes. Take the great ribs of a neck of mutton and chop them asunder, and wash them well. Then put them in a platter one by another, and set them on a chafingdish of charcoals. Cover them and turn them now and then, and so let them stew till they are half cooked. [No liquid is mentioned, despite the word 'stew', so one imagines the meat is being seared to keep in the flavour.] Then take parsley, thyme, marjoram and onions, and chop them very small. Cast upon the steaks, and add one spoonful of verjuice, and two or three spoonfuls of wine, a little butter and marrow. Let them boil till the mutton is tender, and cast thereon a little pepper. If your broth is too sharp, put in a little sugar.'

[The amount of liquid seems small for a broth or stew.]

MUTTON OR VEAL POT PUDDING
Thomas Dawson's *The Second part of The Good Huswifes Jewell*, 1597
'To make a Pudding in a pot. Take a piece of a leg of mutton or veal and parboil it well. Then shred it very fine, with as much suet as there is mutton. Season it with a little pepper and salt. Add cloves and mace, with a good deal of cinnamon and ginger. Then put it in a little pot, and add a good quantity of currants and prunes, and 2 or 3 dates cut longways. Let it seethe softly with a little verjuice upon sops, and so serve it with sugar.'

MUTTON WITH MALLOWES OR TURNEPS
Thomas Dawson's *The good Huswifes Handmaide for the Kitchin*, 1594
'To boil Mutton with Mallowes or Turneps. Take a neck of mutton, cut it in ribs, and put it in a pot with a good quantity of beef broth, and make it boil. Then take your turnips or mallows [marsh mallow roots/stalks] and cut them in pieces, of the bigness of your mutton. Then put into your pot a little pepper, and so let them stew till they are very tender, then take them off, and serve them upon sops.'

MUTTON, BACON AND SPINACH BROTH
Thomas Dawson's *The good Huswifes Handmaide for the Kitchin*, 1594
'To boil Mutton with Spinage. Take your neck of mutton and cut it in pieces, and put it into a fair pot, with a good quantity of mutton broth, and make it boil. Then take sweet [unsalted] bacon, and cut it to the bigness of your finger, and of the same length, and put it in your pot, 6 or

7 pieces. Then take 3 good handfuls of spinach, wash it very clean, and wring the water from it. Cut it small, and put it into the pot, with a little pepper and salt. Look that you have no more broth than will cover your meat. Let it stew very softly till it is tender, then serve it upon sops.'

HODGEPOT OF MUTTON OR BEEF

Thomas Dawson's *The good Huswifes Handmaide for the Kitchin*, 1594

'How to make Hodgepot. Boil a neck of mutton, or a fat rump of beef, and when it is well boiled, take the best of the broth, and put it into a pipkin [a small metal or earthenware pot with a handle]. Put a good many onions to it, two handfuls of marigold flowers, and a handful of parsley fine picked, and grossly shredded, and not too small. And so boil them in the broth, and thicken it with strained bread, adding gross beaten pepper, and a spoonful of vinegar. Let it boil somewhat thick, and so lay it upon your meat.'

[A hodgepodge or hotchpotch has come to mean a random selection of things. People of less opulent means, in an attempt to emulate the wealthy, also wished to season their foods, but were far more likely to use local herbs than imported spices. Balinese long peppers were the first peppers imported into Europe and were used in many Tudor dishes. Hodgepot was usually a mutton broth or stew, with vegetables, similar to the Welsh national dish, *cawl*. The origin appears to have been from the Old French *hocher* (to shake) and pot. Thus ingredients were mixed or shaken up in a large cooking pot. This expression has been corrupted to hodgepodge or hotchpotch over the years. In Anglo-French it was used to describe a dish made in a single pot in which many ingredients were mixed. During the thirteenth century, it came to refer to the process of gathering property and sharing equally cargo that had been damaged and strewn about after the collision of two ships. Both ships were to blame, so the salvage was shared jointly between the owners. The remaining goods were, by the process of hotchpot, divided equally between the owners of the two vessels, based on the premise that both ships contributed to the loss. The term is now synonymous with confusion and disorder, a jumble.]

MUTTON HOTPOT
Thomas Dawson's *The Second part of The Good Huswifes Jewell*, 1597
'To make a pie in a pot. Take the leanest part of a leg of mutton and mince it small, with a piece of the kidney of mutton. Then put it into an earthen pot, adding a ladleful or two of mutton broth, and a little wine. Add a handful each of prunes and raisins, or barberries. Let them boil together, adding half an orange, if you have any. Season it with salt, pepper, cloves, mace and saffron and so serve it.'
[The origin of hotpot may well have been hodgepot; see above.]

A GILLY OF FLESHE – RABBIT, PIGEON, KID, CHICKEN AND CALFSFOOT WITH BROTH
A Noble Boke off Cookry ffor a Prynce Houssolde or eny other estately houssolde, c, 1468
'A gilly of fleshe. To make a gilly of flesh, take rabbits and flay them, and scald pigeons. Chop them and flay of the skin. Scald chickens and chop kids and put all together, and boil it in red wine. Then take it up and lay it in a clean cloth. Dry the pieces of the kid, pigeons and rabbits and couch them in dish and chop chickens and add thereto. Then set the chickens in a cold place where it may stand still [i.e. resting] Then set the broth to the fire again and look it be well strained so that

no fat can abide thereon. Then take scalded calves' feet and lay them in the same broth, till they be tender. And look the broth be clean skimmed. Season it up with salt and serve it.' [This is a slightly early recipe, but would have been served in Tudor times.]

MUTTON OR BEEFE PYES
A. W.'s *A Book of Cookrye*, 1584 and 1591
'For Pyes of Mutton or Beefe. Shred your meat and suet together fine. Season it with cloves, mace, pepper, some saffron, great raisins, currants and prunes, and so put it into your pies.'

MUTTON OR BIEFE PYES
A Proper New Booke of Cookery, 1545 and 1575
'To make Pyes of Mutton or Biefe. The mutton or beef must be finely minced and seasoned with pepper and salt, with a little saffron to colour it. Add a good quantity of suet or marrow, a little vinegar, prunes, great raisins and dates. Take the fattest of the broth of powdered beef, and if you will have *paste royall* [expensive pastry], take butter and yolks of eggs, & so temper the flower to make the pastry.'
[Powdered beef is featured in the diary of Samuel Pepys for 22 February 1660: 'To my father's to dinner, where nothing but a small dish of powdered beef and dish of carrots; they being all busy to get things ready for my brother John to go to-morrow.'

Powdered beef was not dry powdered, but 'sprinkled or seasoned with salt or spice for future use'. This implies something like what we would today call corned beef, beef which has been treated or preserved with 'corns' of salt. The meaning of corn is a coarse grain or particle.]

5. Tudor-era woodcuts of a shepherd and herdsman. Lambs were rarely eaten as they were too valuable as a source of wool and for breeding more sheep. Sheep were only generally slaughtered at the end of their useful life; cattle were slaughtered in October. Both sheep and cattle were vastly smaller than today's breeds.

SALAMAGUNDY or SALMAGUNDI
Elizabethan tradition

'A Crash Test Dummies record refers to Solomon Grundy, who in the old nursery rhyme was "born on Monday, christened on Tuesday ... died on Sunday, that was the end of Solomon Grundy". The obscure origin of the name was *salamagundy*, for which there are many recipes. Its origin is the French *salemine*, meaning highly salted or seasoned. The French then ate *salmigondis*, a communal meat stew to which any available vegetables were added. The basic variety for sailors was Poor John (salt fish) boiled with onions [which could keep at sea]. It could also include chopped meat, eggs and anchovies, whatever was available, in fact. In later years the most luxurious version had meat, turtle, fish and shellfish marinated in spices, herbs, garlic, palm hearts, spiced wine and oil, and served with cabbage, grapes, olives, pickled onions and hard-boiled eggs. Botting described it as having meats that were "roasted, chopped into chunks and marinated in spiced wine, then combined with cabbage, anchovies, pickled herring, mangoes, hard-boiled eggs, palm hearts, onions, olives, grapes and any other pickled vegetables which were available. The whole would then be highly seasoned with garlic, salt, pepper and mustard seed, and doused with oil and vinegar – and served with drafts of beer and rum." Reinhardt describes it thus for privateers in the Caribbean: "Included might be any or all of the following: turtle meat, fish, pork, chicken, corned beef, ham, duck, and pigeon. The meats would be roasted, chopped into pieces and marinated in spied wine, then mixed with cabbage, anchovies, pickled herring, mangoes, hard-boiled eggs, palm hearts, onions, olives, grapes, and any other pickled vegetable available. The entire concoction would then be highly seasoned with

garlic, salt, pepper, and mustard seed and soaked with oil and vinegar." The strong seasonings and vegetables helped suppress scurvy.'
[From *The Pirate Handbook* by Terry Breverton]

LADY ELINOR FETTIPLACE'S MINCE PIES
Elinor Fettiplace's *Receipt Book*, 1604
'Parboil your mutton, then take as much suet as meat, and mince both small. Then add mace, nutmegs, cinnamon, sugar, orange peels, currants, great raisins and a little rose water. Add all these to the meat. Beat your spices & orange peel very small, and mingle your fruit and spices all together with the meat. Bake it. Put as many currants as meat, and twice as much sugar as salt. Add some ginger and let the suet be beef suet, for it is better than mutton suet.'

MUTTON WITH CARRETS
Thomas Dawson's *The good Huswifes Handmaide for the Kitchin*, 1594
'To boil mutton with Carrets. Take a breast or neck of mutton, cut it to the bigness of your thumb, and put it into an earthenware pot with fair water, and make it seethe. Then take carrot roots, and scrape them clean, and cut them of the bigness of your mutton, and let them seethe. Then put in half a handful of stripped thyme, as much of savoury and hyssop, and a little salt and Pepper. Let them seethe till your mutton and roots are very tender, then serve them upon sops [bread].'
[Carrots in Tudor times were white, cream, yellow or purple. A town in southern France, Arausio, founded by the Romans in 35 BC and named after a Celtic water god,

was pronounced Aurenja. That became 'orange' when the French conflated *naranj* with *or*. When William the Silent from Nassau inherited the commune of Orange in 1544, he became Prince William of Orange. He led the Dutch in revolt against the Spanish in the late 1500s, and was assassinated in 1584, but they eventually won their independence in the form of the Dutch Republic. At this time, the Dutch were primarily known as carrot farmers, and grew carrots in the traditional hues of purple, yellow and white. In the seventeenth century, a strain of carrot was developed that contained higher amounts of betacarotene; it was the first orange carrot. Dutch carrot farmers started growing the new orange carrots in honour of William of Orange, and the traditional, more colourful carrots were thrown aside for these newly fashionable orange carrots.]

MUTTON WITH COLEWORTS

Thomas Dawson's *The good Huswifes Handmaide for the Kitchin*, 1594

'To boil Mutton with Colworts. Take a neck of fat mutton, and cut your ribs, and broil them upon a girdiron till they be half cooked. Then put them in a fair earthenware pot, with a good quantity of beef broth, and make them boil. Then take two handfuls of coleworts [*brassica*], and wash them clean. Beat them in pieces, and add them to your mutton, with a ladleful of the fat of your beef broth, and a little pepper and salt. And so let them stew till they are very tender. Put them upon sops. Put no salt in till the meat is ready to be taken out.'

SPANISH BALLES – SHEEP TENNIS BALLS IN BEEF BROTH

Thomas Dawson's *The good Huswifes Handmaide for the Kitchin*, 1594

'To make Spanish balles. Take a piece of a leg of mutton, and pare away the skin from the flesh. Chop the flesh very small. Then take marrow of beef, and cut it as big as a hazel nut. Take as much of marrow in quantity as you have of flesh, and put both in a fair platter. Add some salt and 8 yolks of eggs, and stir them well together. Then take a little earthenware pot, and put in it a pin, and a half of beef broth that is not salted, or else mutton broth and make it seethe. Then make balls of your mixture, and put them in the boiling broth one after another, and let them stew softly for the space of two hours. Then lay them on sops, 3 or 4 in a dish, and ladle the uppermost of the broth upon the sops, and make your balls as big as tennis balls.'

BALLES OF MUTTON

Thomas Dawson's *The good Huswifes Handmaide for the Kitchin*, 1594

'To make balles of Mutton. Take your Mutton and mince it very fine with suet. Then season it with sugar, cinnamon, ginger, cloves and mace*, salt and raw eggs. Mix it in round balls. Let your broth seethe before you put them in. Make your broth with currants, quartered dates, whole mace and salt. Thicken it with yolks of eggs and verjuice, and serve it upon sops.'

*In many recipes, cloves and mace are bracketed together, indicating that this may be a premade mixture of the two spices.

BOILED MUTTON AND CHICKENS
Thomas Dawson's *The Good Huswifes Jewell*, 1596
'To boile mutton and Chyckens. Take your mutton and chickens and set upon the fire with fair water. When it is well scummed, take two handfuls of cabbage, lettuce, a handful of currants, a good piece of butter, the juice of 2 or 3 lemons, a good deal of grosse pepper and a good piece of sugar. Let them seethe all well together, then take 3 or 4 yolks of hard roasted eggs together, and strain them with part of your broth. Let them seethe for an hour. Serve your broth with meat upon sippets [pieces of toast].'

BOILED MUTTON FOR SUPPER
Thomas Dawson's *The Second part of The Good Huswifes Jewell*, 1597
'To boil Mutton for Supper. Take carrot roots, and cut them an inch long. Take a handful of parsley and thyme half chopped, and put into the pot with the mutton, and so let them boil, being seasoned with salt and pepper, and so serve it forth.'
[One wonders why mutton is not now a popular meat – it is brilliant for wholesome stews if well skimmed and cooked for a long time.]

MUTTON IN WHITE BROTH
A Proper New Booke of Cookery, 1545 and 1575
'To make a white brothe. Take a neck of mutton and fair water, and set it upon the fire, and scum it clean. Let it boil half away. Then take forth of the broth two ladlefuls, and put them in a platter. Then chop two handfuls of parsley not too small, and let this boil with the mutton. Then take 12 eggs, and the said two ladlefuls of broth and verjuice, & strain them altogether. Then season your broth with

salt, and a little before you go to dinner, add all these to your mutton. Stir it well, and serve it forth with sops.'

MUTTON [AND OPTIONAL CHICKEN] AND GREENS STEW
A Proper New Booke of Cookery, 1545 and 1575
'Another broth with long wortes. Take mutton and fair water, and let them boil upon the fire. Then take lettuce or spinach, and add and if you wish, to boil therewith 2 or 3 chickens. Add salt & verjuice after your discretion and serve forth, the flesh under, the herbs above [lettuce and spinach were counted as 'herbs'].

MINCED MUTTON AND ORANGE FOR A PIE
Thomas Dawson's *The Good Huswifes Jewell*, 1596
'To boile pie meate. Take a leg of mutton, and mince it very finely with suet and seethe it in a little pan or an earthenware pot with butter. Season it with cloves, mace, great raisins, prunes and salt, and serve it in a dish. And if you will, put in some juie of oranges and lay half an orange upon it.'

BOILED MUTTON WITH HERBS
Thomas Dawson's *The good Huswifes Handmaide for the Kitchin*, 1594
'To boil Mutton with Endive, Borage, or Lettice, or any kinde of herbes that may serve thereunto. When your mutton is well boiled, take the best of the broth, and put it in a pipkin [a small earthenware pan or pot]. Add a handful of endive, borage, or what herbs you wish, and cast upon a few currants, and let them boil well. Add a piece of upper crust of white bread. Season it with pepper

gross beaten, and a little verjuice, and a little sugar, and so pour it upon your meat.'

MUTTON, VEAL OR KID POTTAGE WITH WHOLE HERBS

Gervase Markham's *Countrey Contentments, or, The English Hus-wife*, 1615

'Mutton pottage with whole herbs. Take mutton, veal or kid, break the bones but do not cut up the flesh. Wash, and put in a pot with water. When ready to boil and well skimmed, add a handful or two of small oatmeal. Take whole lettuce (the best inner leaves), whole spinach, whole endive, whole chicory, whole leaves of cauliflower or the inward parts of white cabbage, with 2 or 3 onions. Put all into the pot until cooked. Season with salt and as much verjuice as will only turn the taste of the pottage. Serve, covering the meat with whole herbs and adorning the dish with sippets [croutons].'

STEWED MUTTON, CHICKEN OR SPARROWS

A Proper New Booke of Cookery, 1545 and 1575

'For to stewe Mutton. Take a neck of mutton and a breast to make the broth strong, and then scum it cleane [skim, remove the scum]. When it has boiled a while, take part of the broth, and put it into another pot. Add to this a pound of raisins, and let them boil till tender. Then strain a little bread with the raisins and the broth all together. Then chop thyme, savory and parsley with other small herbs, and add to the mutton. Then put in the strained raisins with whole prunes, cloves and mace, pepper, saffron and a little salt. And if you wish, you may stew a chicken in the same way, or else sparrows, "or such other little byrdes".'

FRENCH POTTAGE

Thomas Dawson's *The good Huswifes Handmaide for the Kitchin*, 1594

'How to make a French pottage. Take the ribs of mutton, chop them small, the bones and all, with the flesh in square pieces. Then take carrot roots, and for lack of them, onions, or both together. If you wish, use instead or as well herbs [greens in this instance], such as you like. Seethe all these together, and when you will serve it, season your pot with a little cinnamon, pepper and salt, and so serve it forth.'

BOILED LEG OF MUTTON WITH LEMONS

Thomas Dawson's *The good Huswifes Handmaide for the Kitchin*, 1594

'To boil a leg of Mutton with Lemons. When your mutton is half boiled, take it up, cut it in small pieces. Put it into a pipkin, and cover it closely, and add the best of the broth, as much as shall cover your mutton. Add your lemons being sliced very thinly, and quartered, and currants. Put in pepper gross beaten, and let them boil together, and when they are well boiled, season it with a little verjuice, sugar, pepper gross beaten, and a little sanders [colouring], and so lay it in fine dishes upon sops. It will make three messe [servings] for the table.'

[The lemon with mutton helps take away any greasiness.]

LAMB BAKE MEATES PIES

Thomas Dawson's *The Good Huswifes Jewell*, 1596

'To make bake meates. Take a leg of lamb, and cut out all the flesh, and save the skin whole. Then mince it fine, put in grated bread, and some eggs white and all, and some dates and currants. Then season with some pepper, cinnamon, ginger, some nutmegs and caraway seeds, and a little cream. Temper it all together, then put it into the leg of the lamb again, and let it bake a little before you put it into your pie. When you have put it into your pie, then put in a little of the pudding about it. When it is almost baked, then put in verjuice, sugar and sweet butter, and so serve it.'

KID IN A COFFIN

Thomas Dawson's *The Good Huswifes Jewell*, 1596

'To bake a Kidde. Take your kid and parboil him, and wash it in verjuice and saffron, & season it with pepper, salt, & a little mace. Then lay it in your coffin, with sweet [unsalted] butter and the liquor it was seasoned in, and so bake it.'

ROASTED VENISON

A Proper New Booke of Cookery, 1545 and 1575

'To roste Venison. Roasted venison must have vinegar, sugar, cinnamon, and butter, and boiled upon a chafingdish with charcoal, but the sauce may not be too tart. Then lay the venison upon the sauce.'

BAKED VINEGARED RED DEARE

Thomas Dawson's *The good Huswifes Handmaide for the Kitchin*, 1594

'To bake Red Deare. You must take a handful of fennel, a handful of winter savory*, a handful of rosemary, a handful of thyme, and a handful of bay leaves. When your liquor seethes [comes to the boil] that you parboil your venison in, put in your herbs also. Parboil your venison till it is half cooked, then take it out. Lay it upon a fair board that the water may run from it. Then take a knife and prick it full of holes, and while it is warm, have a fair tray with vinegar therein, and so put your venison therein from morning until night. Every now and then turn it upside down, and then at night have your coffin [pastry case] ready. This done, season it with cinnamon, nutmegs and ginger, pepper and salt. When you have seasoned it, put it into your coffin, and put a good quantity of sweet butter into it. Then put it into the oven at night, when you go to bed. In the morning draw it forth, and put in a saucer full of vinegar into your pie at a hole above in the top of it, so that the vinegar may run into every place of it. Then stop the hole again, and turn the bottom upward, and so serve it.'

*This is *Satureja montana*, different to summer savory, *Satureja hortensis*, which the Tudors also used. Their repertoire of spices and vegetables is only being replicated in this author's lifetime in English cuisine. For the upper classes at least, ginger, borage, marjoram, cinnamon, nutmeg, fennel, thyme, pennyroyal, rosemary, mint, liquorice, saffron, parsley, cloves, canella, saunders, hyssop, sage, mace, rosewater, caraway and bay were common seasonings. Skirret, artichoke, sorrel, nettles, chickweed, endive and other excellent vegetables and greens were also in common usage at top tables.

BAKED VENISON (1)
A Proper New Booke of Cookery, 1545 and 1575
'To bake Venison. Take nothing but pepper and salt, but let it have enough, and if the venison is lean, baste with lard while cooking.'

BAKED VENISON (2)

Thomas Dawson's *The good Huswifes Handmaide for the Kitchin*, 1594

'To bake Venison. Parboil your venison, then season it with pepper and salt, somewhat gross beaten, and a little ginger, and good store of sweet butter. Add these when the venison is tender baked. Add to it half a dozen spoonfuls of claret wine, and shake it well together.'

BAKED VENISON OR MUTTON

Thomas Dawson's *The good Huswifes Handmaide for the Kitchin*, 1594

'To bake Venison, or Mutton in stead of Venison. Take lean venison or mutton, and take out all the sinews. Then chop your flesh very small, and season it with a little pepper and salt, beaten cloves, and a good handful of fennel seeds. Mingle them all together. Then take your lard, and cut it to the bigness of a goose quill, and the length of your finger, and put it in a dish of vinegar, & all to wash it therein. Then take oatmeal as it comes from the mill, and make paste with cold water, and see that it is very stiff. Then take a sheet, and make a laying of the minced flesh upon the sheet, of the breadth that your lard is of length, then make a laying of your lard upon your meat. Let your lard be one from another, the breadth of one of the pieces of the lard, and so make four layings of lard, and three layings of meat one upon the another. Press it down with your hands as hard as you can without breaking the pastry. Cast in a handful of pepper and salt & beaten cloves, and close up your pastry, & let it bake two hours.'

HUMBLE PYE – DEER INTESTINES PIE

Thomas Dawson's *The Good Huswifes Jewell*, 1596

'To make a Pye of Humbles. Take your humbles being parboiled, and chop them very small with a good quantity of mutton suet, and half a handful of the herbs following – thyme, marjoram, borage, parsley and a little rosemary. Season the same being chopped, with pepper, cloves and mace, and so close your pie and bake it.'

[The origin of the term 'humble pie' is that 'umble' or 'umbles' were the intestines of deer. The master ate pie made with venison – muscle meat – while the servants ate the leftovers, 'umble pie'.]

RED DEERE, FALLOW-DEERE, SWANNE OR RAMME MUTTON COFFINS – VENISON, SWAN OR MUTTON PIES

Gervase Markham's *Countrey Contentments, or, The English Hus-wife*, 1615

'When you bake red deer, you shall first parboil it and take out the bones. Then you shall, if it be lean, lard it. If fat save the charge. Then put it into a press to squeeze out the blood. Then for a night lay it in a meare* sauce made of vinegar, small drinke [weak ale] and salt. Then taking it forth, season it well with pepper finely beaten, and salt well mixed together. See that you lay good store thereof, both upon and in every open and hollow place of the venison. But by no means cut any slashes to put in the pepper, for it will of itself sink fast enough into the flesh, and be more pleasant in the eating. Then having raised the coffin, lay in the bottom a thick course of butter, then lay the flesh thereon and cover it all over with butter. Bake it as much as if you did bake great brown bread. Then when you draw it from the oven, melt more butter with 3 or 4 spoonfuls of vinegar, and twice as much Claret wine, and at a vent hole on the top of the lid pour in the same, till it can receive no more. And so let it stand and cool. And in this way you may bake fallow-deer, or swan, or whatsoever else you please to keep cold, the meare sauce only being left out which is only proper to red deer. And if to your meare sauce you add a little turnesole, and therein steep beef, or ram mutton. You may also in the same manner take the first for red deer venison, and the latter for fallow, and a very good judgement shall not be able to say otherwise than that it is of itself perfect venison, both in taste, colour, and the manner of cutting.'

*Meere, or meare, sauce accompanied venison and was also made from red wine and wine vinegar.

[Turnsole is a food colouring made from the heliotrope plant. Gerard's *Herbal* calls it *Heliotropium minus* or Small Torne-sole and states, 'With the small Tornsole they in France doe die linnen rags and clouts into a perfect purple colour, wherewith cookes and confectioners doe colour iellies, wines, meates, and sundry confectures.' Now known as *Chrozophora tinctoria*, it has many common names. One of the most detailed medieval recipes in the late fourteenth-century Neapolitan *De Arte Illuminandi* states that the seeds are to be picked carefully off their stems, and squeezed in a linen cloth to extract the juice. Pieces of clean linen or muslin, having first been soaked in a lye of water and quicklime (calcium oxide), washed and dried, are then soaked in the turnsole juice for a day and a night. Then in a dark, damp place one lays rich garden soil on a tray and has a healthy man who has been copiously drinking wine urinate on the earth. The juice-soaked cloths are then placed on a drying rack in the fumes of the urine and left for several days, to expose the cloths to an alkaline environment and push up the pH level. This fixes the colour in the blue/purple tones. A description in 1839 by the French writer N. Joly explains that turnsole fruits were squeezed in a press, the juice mixed with urine, and the cloths soaked, dried and then sandwiched in hay which was placed over deep beds of fermenting horse dung. They were re-soaked and dried over dung again to achieve the desired dark purple.]

THE SYDES OF A DERE OF HYE GRECE ROSTYDE – ROASTED VENISON
Gentyll Manly Cokere, MS Pepys 1047, *c.* 1490
'The Sydes of a Dere of hye Grece Rostyde. Wash the sides of a deer. Remove the fillets & put them on a spit and roast them. Put them on the spit outer-wards and a loaf of bread crosswise. Take red wine, powder of pepper and salt, and baste them with this, until done. Have a charger underneath to keep the drippings. Baste again with the drippings then serve it forth.'

LONG-LIFE COUNTERFEIT VENISON PASTIE
Thomas Dawson's *The Good Huswifes Jewell*, 1596
'To make fillets of beefe or clods instead of red Deare. First take your beef, and lard it very thick, and then season it with pepper, salt, cinnamon, ginger, cloves and mace in a good store. Use a great deal more quantity of pepper and salt than you would a piece of venison. Put it in covered pastry, and when it is baked, take vinegar and sugar, cinnamon and ginger, and put it in. Shake the pasty, and stop it close, and let it stand almost a fortnight before you cut it up.'

MEAT IN WHITE BROTH WITH ORANGE AND ALMONDS

Thomas Dawson's *The Good Huswifes Jewell*, 1596

'To make white broth with Almonds. First look that your meat be clean washed, and then set it on the fire. When it boils skim it clean. Put some salt into the pot, then take rosemary, thyme, hyssop and marjoram, and bind them together in a *bouquet garni*. Put into the pot. Take a dish of sweet butter, and put it into the pot amongst your meat. Take some whole mace, and bind in a cloth, and put them into the pot with a quantity of verjuice. After that take a quantity of almonds, as shall serve the turn. Blanch them, and beat them in a mortar, and then strain them with the broth your meat is in. And when these almonds are strained put them in a pot by themselves with some sugar, a little ginger, and also a little rosewater, and then stir it while it boils. After that take some slices of oranges, without the kernels, and boil them with the broth of the pot upon a chafingdish of charcoal, with a little sugar. Then have some sippets [toast or bread soaked in gravy] ready in a platter. Serve the meat upon them, and put not your almonds in till it be ready to be served.'

BAKED RABBIT, VEAL OR MUTTON

Thomas Dawson's *The Second part of The Good Huswifes Jewell*, 1597

'To bake a Connie, Veal, or Mutton. Take a rabbit and parboil it almost enough, then mince the flesh of it very fine. Take with it 3 yolks of hard eggs, and mince with it, then lay another rabbit in your pie being parboiled. Add your minced meat with it, being seasoned with cloves, mace, ginger, saffron, pepper & salt, with two dishes of sweet butter mixed with it. Lay upon your rabbit barberries, gooseberries, grapes or the small raisins, and so bake it.'

MINCED HARE PIE
Thomas Dawson's *The Good Huswifes Jewell*, 1596
'For to bake a Hare. Take your hare and parboil him, and mince him, and then beat him in a mortar very fine, liver and all if you will. Season it with all kind of spices and salt. And do him together with the yolks of 7 or 8 eggs, and when you have made him up together, draw lard very thick through him, and mingle them altogether, and put him in a pie, and put in butter before you close him up.'

ROASTED 'EARS-ON' HARE
Thomas Dawson's *The Good Huswifes Jewell*, 1596
'To roast an Hare. You must not cut off her head, feet nor ears, but make a pudding in her belly, and put paper about her ears that they burn not. When the hare is roasted, you must take cinnamon, ginger, and grated bread, & you must make a very sweet sauce, and you must put in barberries and let them boil together.'

ROASTED RABBET IN SAWCE FOR KING HENRY VIII
John Partridge's *The Treasurie of commodious Conceits*, 1573
'A Sawce for a rosted Rabbet: to King Henry the eight. Take a handful of washed parsley, mince it small. Boil it with butter & verjuice upon a chafingdish. Season it

with sugar and a little pepper grose beaten [ground black pepper]. When it is ready, put in a few fine crumbs of white bread, put it in amongst the other. Let it boil again till it be standing. Then lay it in a platter, like the breadth of three fingers, lay on each side one roasted rabbit (or more) and so serve them.'

STUFFED 'EARS-ON' RABBIT
Thomas Dawson's *The good Huswifes Handmaide for the Kitchin*, 1594
'To boil a Conie with a Pudding in his belly. Take your rabbit and flea [skin] him, and leave on the ears, and wash it fair. Take grated bread, sweet suet minced fine, currants, and some fine herbs, pennyroyal, winter savory, parsley, spinach or beets, sweet marjoram. Chop your herbs fine, and season it with cloves, mace and sugar, and a little cream, salt, yolks of eggs, and dates minced fine. Then mingle all your stuff together, and put it into your rabbit's belly, and sow it up with a thread. For the broth, take mutton broth, when it is boiled a little, and put it in, then put in gooseberries or else grapes, currants, sweet butter, verjuice, salt, grated bread, and sugar a little. When it is boiled, lay it in a dish with sops, and so serve it.'

RABBIT IN MUTTON BROTH
Thomas Dawson's *The Good Huswifes Jewell*, 1596
'To boile Conies. Take a rabbit and parboil it a little, then take a good handful of parsley and a few sweet herbs, and the yolks of 4 hard eggs. Chop them all together, then put in pepper, and a few currants. Fill the rabbit's belly full of butter. Then prick her head between her hind legs

and break her not, and put her into a fair earthenware pot with mutton broth, and the rest of the mixture roll it up round and put it in withall. And so boil them well together, and serve it with sops.'

BIRD, RABBIT OR MUTTON BROTH
The Good Hous-wiues Treasurie, 1588
'How to make broth either for Birdes, Rabits or Mutton. Take a short marow bone and cleave it asunder, and take out the marrow. Then seethe the bone in fair water. Then take a porringer [a shallow bowl about six inches across] full of the uppermost of the broth [and] half a pint of white wine. Put in a pipkin, then put in your meat, and if it be birds or rabbits, put in their bellies parsley, butter, mace, whole pepper, sugar, cinnamon & currants. Leave on the birds' heads, and put in but a little of all these things aforenamed, but if it be mutton then put all these into the broth, besides the fruit that is put in, put in a little grated bread, bind in a few herbs. Half an hour before you take up the broth, put in 10 roots of white endive. Cut off but a little of the root or else it will fall asunder, then put in your marrow, and let it seethe no longer than till it be thoroughly hot.'

RABBIT PIE
Thomas Dawson's *The Good Huswifes Jewell*, 1596
'To bake Connies. Have fine pastry ready, wash your rabbits, and parboil them. Then cast them into the cold water. Then season them with salt and ginger, lay them into the pastry and upon them lay leached lard, close them, and bake them.'

BLACK PUDDING (1)

Thomas Dawson's *The Good Huswifes Jewell*, 1596

'To make blacke puddings. Take great oatmeal and lay it in milk to steep. Then take sheeps' blood and add to it, and take ox white and mince into it. Then take a few sweet herbs and 2 or 3 leek blades, and chop them very small, and then put into it the yolks of some eggs. Season it with cinnamon, ginger, cloves, mace, pepper and salt, and so fill them.'

['Sweet herbs' referred to those herbs that could be eaten raw, or could be added directly to stews and pottages. All other herbs were 'potherbs' and required blanching before consumption. Those most usually employed for purposes of cooking, such as the flavouring of soups, sauces, forcemeats, etc., were thyme, sage, mint, marjoram, savory and basil. They were sometimes tied into a bunch, much like a *bouquet garni*, but this latter method was more likely to be used for pot herbs, to remove from the dish prior to serving. Sweet herbs were typically soft-leaved herbs used in enhancing the flavour of a dish, while 'savoury herbs' or 'pot herbs' with strong, penetrating flavours were used to flavour stews cooked in pots. Sweet herbs tend to be annual in nature, are not woody and have aromatic oils that give a pleasant fragrance when crushed. They break down into the stock and do not need to be removed. They can often be eaten raw, and can be added to salads to improve the flavour.]

BLACK PUDDING (2)

The Good Hous-wiues Treasurie, 1588

'How to make blacke Puddinges. Take oatmeal and steep it in sodden milk, then take hog suet & good herbs and chop them small, then put in fennel seed, pepper and salt.'

WHITE PUDDINGES
The Good Hous-wiues Treasurie, 1588

'How to make white Puddinges. Take grated bread, currants, yolks of eggs, nutmegs, cinnamon, and some sugar, salt and beef suet. Temper them with cream.'

LIVERING PUDDINGES
The Good Hous-wiues Treasurie, 1588

'How to make Livering Puddinges. Take the liver of a hogge, and give it 3 or 4 warms [bring to the boil] over the fire. Then either grate it or chop it very small, and take a little grated bread and two eggs well beaten, whites and all, and currants, nutmegs, pepper, salt and hog suet.'

6. A Tudor-period woodcut of a cook in a kitchen. Most depictions of this time show an overweight cook.

PUDDING BALLS
Thomas Dawson's *The good Huswifes Handmaide for the Kitchin*, 1594
'To make Puddinges. Take grated bread, the yolks of 6 eggs, a little cinnamon and salt, currants, one minced date, and the suet of mutton minced small. Knead all these together, and make them up in little balls, cook them on a chafingdish with a little butter and vinegar. Cast cinnamon and sugar thereon, and so serve them in.'

GALLANTINE FOR FLESH OR FISH
Thomas Dawson's *The Second part of The Good Huswifes Jewell*, 1597
'To make gallantine for flesh or fish. Take brown bread and burn it black in the toasting of it. Take them and lay them in a little wine and vinegar. When they have soaked a while, then strain them. Season with cinnamon, ginger, pepper and salt, then set it on a chafingdish with charcoal, and let it cook till it be thick, and then serve it in saucers.'

STUED BROTH FOR MEAT OR FISH
A Proper New Booke of Cookery, 1545 and 1575
'To make a stued broth for Capons, mutton, biefe, or other hotte meate, and also a broth for all maner of freshe fishe. Take half a handful of rosemary and as much of thyme, and bind it on a bundle with thread after it is washed. Put it in the pot, after the pot has been clean skimmed, and let it boil a while. Then cut sops of white bread, and put them in a great charger [large dish], and put on the same scalding broth, until it is soaked enough.

Then strain it through a strainer, with a quantity of wine or good ale, so that it be not too tart. And when it is strained, pour it in a pot, and then put in your raisins and prunes, and so let them boil till the meat be cooked. If the broth be too sweet, put in more wine, or else a little vinegar.'

Note: For any mutton dish you may substitute lamb. Also, using stale bread for sippets (pieces of toast) upon which to present the meal is a good way of using up bread.

7. Woodcut illustrations from 1574 depicting a chicken being butchered and a rabbit on its warren. All monasteries and gentry in the country had their own warrens.

8. Elizabeth I enjoying a picnic following a hunt. Wine and beer is available, along with baskets of roasted fowl for refreshments.

3

Fowl Foods

LIVE BLACKBIRD, RABBIT, FROG, DOG OR DWARF PIE
Epulario, or The Italian Banquet, 1598 translation of 1516 edition

> Sing a song of six-pence, a pocket full of rye
> Four and twenty blackbirds, baked in a pie
> When the pie was opened, the birds began to sing.
> Now wasn't that a tasty dish to set before the king!

'To make Pies that the Birds may be alive in them, and flie out when it is cut up. Take the coffin of a great pie or pastry, and in the bottom thereof make a hole as big as your fist, or bigger if you will. Let the sides of the coffin be somewhat higher than ordinary pies, which done put it full of flour and bake it. Being baked, open the hole in the bottom, and take out the flour. Then having a pie of the bigness of the hole in the bottom of the coffin aforesaid, you shall put it into the coffin. Withall put into the said coffin round about the aforesaid pie as many small live birds as the empty coffin will hold, besides the pie aforesaid. And this is to be done at such time as you send the pie to the table, and set before the guests. Where uncovering or cutting up the lid of the great pie, all the birds will flie out, which is to delight and pleasure show to the company. And because they shall not be altogether mocked, you shall cut open the small pie, and in this sort you may make many others, the like you may do with a tart.'

[A sixteenth-century court amusement was to place live birds in a pie as a form of *entremets*. The way Tudors made pie crusts was a little different in that the thick crust could be baked first, and would rise forming a pot, hence the term 'pot pie'. The lid would be removed from the pie, and birds would then be set inside, the lid put back on and then this entertaining dish placed before the host of the party. Thus the birds were not actually cooked in the pie. The Stuart cook Robert May filled such a pie with live frogs to 'make the ladies to skip and shreek'. Not only were birds baked into pies, but rabbits, frogs, dogs and people of restricted growth, who would pop out and recite poetry. At one time a whole little musical group emerged to the delight of the diners. The experimental celebrity chef Heston Blumenthal attempted to recreate the dish for an episode of his television series *Heston's Medieval Feast*. Discovering that blackbirds are a protected species, he altered the recipe to include pigeon. The pie and pie lid were cooked separately and allowed to cool, and live pigeons inserted only moments before presentation. Initial attempts resulted in the pigeons refusing to fly out, but this was solved by using trained homing pigeons to fly to their cages suspended in the ceiling. (*The Tudor Kitchen*, Terry Breverton, 2015)]

APHRODISIAC TART WITH COCK SPARROW BRAINS

Thomas Dawson's *The Good Huswifes Jewell*, 1596

'To make a tarte that is a courage to a man or woman. Take 2 quinces, and 2 or 3 burr [probably common butterbur] roots, and a sweet potato, and peel your potato, and scrape your roots and put them into a quart of wine. Let them boil till they be tender, & put in an ounce of dates. When they be boiled tender, draw them through a strainer, wine and all. Then put in the yolks of 8 eggs, and the brains of 3 or 4 cock sparrows, and strain them into the other. Add a little rosewater, and seethe them all with sugar, cinnamon, ginger, cloves and mace. Put in a little sweet butter, and set it upon a chafingdish of charcoal between two platters, and so let it boil till it be something big.'

[Potatoes were not used in Tudor cuisine, but sweet potatoes were both imported and grown.]

SOPS FOR A CAPON

Thomas Dawson's *The good Huswifes Handmaide for the Kitchin*, 1594

'To make Sops for a Capon. Take toasts of bread, butter, claret wine, and slices of oranges, and lay them upon the toasts, with cinnamon, sugar and ginger.'

SOPS FOR CHICKENS

Thomas Dawson's *The good Huswifes Handmaide for the Kitchin*, 1594

'To make Sops for Chickens. First take butter, and melt it upon a chafingdish with charcoal, and lay in the dish thin toasts of bread. Make sorrel sauce with verjuice and gooseberries, seethe them with a little verjuice and lay them upon.'

TO BOIL TEAL, MALLARD, PIGEON, PORK OR BEEF-TONGUE

Thomas Dawson's *The Second part of The Good Huswifes Jewell*, 1597

'To boil teales, Mallards, pigeons, chines of porke, or Neates tunges all after one sort. Let them be half roasted, stick a few cloves in their breasts, then two or three toasts of bread being burned black, then put them into a little fair water. Immediately take them out again, and strain them with a little wine and vinegar to the quantity of a pint. Put into an earthenware pot, and take 8 or 10 onions sliced small, being fried in a frying pan with a dish of butter. When they are fried, put them into your broth, then take your meat from the spit and put it into the same broth, and so let them boil together for a time, seasoning with salt and pepper.'

MUSTARD, HONEY AND ONION SAUCE FOR A ROASTED MALLARD

Gentyll Manly Cokere, MS Pepys 1047, *c.* 1490

'Sauce for a mawlerd Rosted.'

> Take onyons And mense them wele
> Put sum yn thy mawlerd so have the sele
> And mynce more Onyons I the ken
> With the grece of the mawlerd seth hit then
> Put ale mustad And hony ther to
> Boyle all to geder tyll hit be enowe.

[Sauce for a Roasted Mallard: Take onions and mince them well / Put some in thy mallard to have good luck / And mince more onions, I teach you / With grease of the mallard boil it then / Add ale, honey and mustard / Boil all together till it be ready.]

TO BOILE LARKES

Thomas Dawson's *The Good Huswifes Jewell*, 1596

'To Boile Larkes. Take sweet bread, & strain it into a pipkin, and set it on the fire. Put in a piece of butter, and skim it as clean as you can. Put in spinach and endive, and cut it a little, and so let it boil. And put in pepper, cloves and mace, cinnamon and ginger, and a little verjuice, and when you serve them up, lay sops in the dish.'

PORRAIE – CHICKEN PATÉ

A Proper New Booke of Cookery, 1545 and 1575

'To make Porraie. Take a capon or a hen, and either beef or mutton to make the broth sweet withall, and boil them all together till they be very tender. Then take the capon or hen out of the pot & take out all his bones, and bray him in a mortar, with 2 pounds of almonds over blanched. Then with the broth of your capon or hen, strain them meetly thick, then put it in a little pot. Season it with a little sugar, sanders [red sandalwood colouring], cloves, mace, and small raisins*. Boil and serve upon sops.'

*Sultanas are 'small raisins'. They are seedless dried grapes, sweet, pale golden in colour and come mainly from Turkey. Compared to raisins, sultanas also easily absorb liquid, but are smaller and slightly sweeter. Sultanas are used in the same ways you'd use raisins. Raisins are larger, and made from any dried white grapes. Currants are dried black seedless grapes originally produced in Greece, and were known as 'raisins of the sun', or raisins of Corinth, or Corance, from where we get the term currants. They are also known as Zante currants. Our blackcurrant, redcurrant and whitecurrant are different fruits, grown on spiky bushes.

COFFIN OF BAKED CHICKINS

John Partridge's *The Treasurie of commodious Conceits*, 1573

'To bake Chickins. Take and truss your chickens, the feet cut off, and put them in the coffin. Then for every chicken put in every pie a handful of gooseberries, & a quantity of butter about every chicken. Then take a good quantity of sugar and cinnamon with sufficient salt. Put them into the pie, and let it bake one hour and a half. When it is baked take the yolk of an egg & half a goblet of verjuice with sufficient sugar sodden together. Put in the pie & serve it.'

CAPONS IN DORRE – CHICKEN IN GOLDEN ALMOND MILK

Gentyll Manly Cokere, MS Pepys 1047, *c.* 1490

'Capons in Dorre. Grind blanched almonds, then temper them up with fair water unto a good milk. And draw it through a strainer into a pot. Add saffron for if thou wish, thou may colour it a little therewith. Add thereto sugar and salt and set it on the fire. Stir it well and when it is at the boiling add a little good wine. Take it from the fire and stir it well, and then take white bread and cut it in the manner of thin brewes. Toast them a little on a roast iron that they be somewhat brown and then dip them a little in wine and toast them better. And add a little milk in dishes and couch 3 or 4 toasts in a dish and pour more milk upon and serve forth. *Probatum est.*' ['It has been proved'. This term was often used by physicians, such as Nicholas Culpeper and the Physicians of Myddfai. In the seventeenth century Hannah Wolley gave us '*Probatum est*. An infallible receipt to increase milk in a woman's breasts. Take chickens and make a broth of them, then add thereunto fennel and parsnip roots, then take the best made butter you can procure, and butter the roots therewith; having done so let her eat heartily, and her expectations will be speedily satisfied.']

STEWED CAPON FOR DINNER

Thomas Dawson's *The Second part of The Good Huswifes Jewell*, 1597

'To stewe a Capon for Dinner. Take a knuckle of veal and boil it with your capon. Add to it prunes, great and small raisons, whole mace, and let it boil together, seasoning it with salt. And so serve it forth.'

TURKIE, GOOSE, PHEASANT OR CAPON COFFINS

Thomas Dawson's *The Good Huswifes Jewell*, 1596

'To bake a Turkie and take out his bones. Take a fat turkey, and after you have scalded him and washed him clean, lay him upon a fair cloth and slit him throughout the back. When you have taken out his garbage, then you must take out his bones as bare as you can. When you have so done wash him clean, then truss him and prick his back together, and so have a fair kettle of seething water and parboil him a little. Then take him up that the water may run clean out from him, and when he is cold, season him with pepper and salt. Then prick him with a few cloves in the breast, and also draw him with lard if you like of it. When you have made your coffin and laid your turkey in it, then you must put some butter in it. And so close him up. In this manner you may bake a goose, a pheasant, or capon.'

TO MAKE PASTE AND TO BAKE CHICKENS

Thomas Dawson's *The good Huswifes Handmaide for the Kitchin*, 1594

'To make paste, and to bake Chickens. Take water, and put in a good piece of butter, and let it seethe as hot as you can blow off your butter into your flour. Break two yolks of eggs, and one white, and put in a good piece of sugar. Colour your pastry with saffron, then shall it be short. Then take your chickens, and season them with pepper, salt, saffron, great raisins, cloves, mace, currants, prunes and dates. Then close them up, and make a little hole in the middle of the lid. Then set the pie in the oven. To make syrup for the same pie, take Malmsey [sweet fortified wine], cream and two yolks of eggs, and beat them together. Add in cinnamon and sugar. When the pie is almost baked, then put in the syrup, and let them bake together.'

9. Food is prepared for a Tudor-era feast; birds are being spitroasted by hand while pages prepare to bring out the first courses. In the background, guests make merry.

BAKED CHEKINS IN LYKE PAEST – FRUIT AND CHICKEN PIE

The Proper Newe Booke of Cookerye, c. 1557

'To bake chekins in lyke paes't. Take your chickens and season them with a little ginger and salt, and put them into your coffins. And add barberries, grapes or gooseberries, and half a dish of butter. Close them up, and set them in the oven, and when they are baked, take the yolks of 6 eggs, and a dishful of verjuice. Draw them through a strainer. Set it upon a chafingdish, then draw from the oven your baked chicken pies and add thereto the eggs and verjuice mixture, and thus serve them hot.'

CAPON WITH ORANGES AFTER MISTRESS DUFFELDS WAY

Thomas Dawson's *The good Huswifes Handmaide for the Kitchin*, 1594

'To boil a Capon with Oranges after Mistress Duffelds way. Take a capon and boil it with veal, or with a marrow bone, or whatever your fancy is. Then take a good quantity of the broth, and put it in an earthenware pot by itself. Add thereto a good handful of currants, and as many prunes, and a few whole maces, and some marie [marrow, rather than rosemary]. Add to this broth a good quantity of white wine or of Claret, and so let them seethe softly together. Then take your oranges, and with a knife scrape of all the filthiness off the outside of them. Then cut them in the middle, and wring out the juice of three or four of them. Put the juice into your broth with the rest of your stuff. Then slice your oranges thinly, and have ready upon the fire a skillet of fair seething water, and put your sliced oranges into the water. When that water is bitter [oranges were bitter at this time], have more ready, and so change them still as long as you can find the great bitterness in the water, which will be six or seven times, or more, if you find need. Then take them from the water, and let that run clean from them. Then put close oranges into your pot with your broth, and so let them stew together till your capon is ready. Then make your sops with this broth, and cast on a little cinnamon, ginger, and sugar, and upon this lay your capon, and some of your oranges upon it, and some of your marie [marrow jelly], and toward the end of the boiling of your broth, put in a little verjuice, if you think best.'

BOYLED PIGEONS WITH RICE – PIGEONS IN RICE PUDDING

Sir Hugh Plat's *Delightes for Ladies*, 1602

'To boyle Pigeons with rice. Boil them in mutton broth, putting sweet herbs in their bellies, then take a little rice and boil it in cream, with a little whole mace. Season it with sugar, lay it thick on their breasts, wringing also the juice of a lemon upon them, and so serve them.'

FRENCH-STYLE BOILED MEATS – PIGEON PUDDINGS

Thomas Dawson's *The Good Huswifes Jewell*, 1596

'To make a boyled meat after the French waies. Take pigeons and lard them, and then put them on a broach [spit], and let them be half roasted. Then take them off the broach, and make a pudding of sweet herbs, of every sort a good handful. Chop ox white amongst the herbs very small. Take the yolks of 5 or 6 eggs and grated bread, and season with pepper, cinnamon, ginger, cloves, mace, sugar and currants, and mingle all together. Then put the stuff on the pigeons round about, and then put the pigeons into the cabbages that be parboiled. Bind the cabbage fast to the pigeons. Then put them into the pot where you mean to boil them, and put in beef broth into them, and cabbages chopped small, and so let them boil. Put in pepper, cloves and mace, and prick the pigeons full of cloves before you put the pudding on them. Add a piece of butter, cinnamon and ginger, and a little vinegar and white wine, and so serve them up. Garnish them with fruit, and serve one in a dish, and when you serve them, up you must put into the dish just a little of the broth.'

STEWED LARKS OR SPARROWES
Thomas Dawson's *The good Huswifes Handmaide for the Kitchin*, 1594

'To stew Larks or Sparrowes. Take of your mutton broth the best, and put it in a pipkin. Add to it a little whole mace, whole pepper, claret wine, marigold leaves, barberries, rosewater, verjuice, sugar and marrow, or else sweet butter. Parboil the larks before, and then boil them in the same broth, and lay them upon sops.'

DUCK OR PORK WITH CABBAGE
Thomas Dawson's *The Second part of The Good Huswifes Jewell*, 1597

'To boil Mallards, Teales, and chines of porke with Cabbadge. First unloose your cabbages, and cut them in three or four quarters, unloosing every leaf for doubt of worms to be in them. Then wash them and put them into a pot of fair water, and let them boil a quarter of an hour. Then take them up, and chop them somewhat great. Then put them into a fair pot with the broth of the mallard and whole pepper, and pepper beaten, with cloves, mace, and salt, and so let them boil together.'

TO BAKE CHICKENS IN SUMMER
Thomas Dawson's *The good Huswifes Handmaide for the Kitchin*, 1594

'To bake Chickens in Summer. Cut off their feet, truss them in the coffins. Then take for every chicken a good handful of gooseberries, and put into the pie with the chickens. Then take a good quantity of butter, and put about every chicken in the pie. Then take a good quantity of cinnamon and ginger, and put it in the pie with salt and let them bake an hour, when they be baked, take for every pie a yolk of an egg, and half a goblet full of verjuice, and a good quantity of sugar, and put them all together into the pie to the chickens, and so serve them.'

TO BAKE CHICKENS IN WINTER
Thomas Dawson's *The good Huswifes Handmaide for the Kitchin*, 1594

'To bake Chickens in Winter. Cut off their feet, and truss them, and put them in the pies. Take to every pie a certain amount of currants or prunes, & and put them in the pie with the chickens. Then take a good quantity of butter to every chicken, and put in the pie. Then take a good quantity of ginger and salt, and season them together, & put them in the pie, let it bake the space of an hour and a half. When baked, take the sauce as is aforesaid, and so serve them in it.'

COCK BRAINS AND ALMOND BROTH FOR SICKE MEN

Thomas Dawson's *The Good Huswifes Jewell*, 1596

'To make strong broth for sicke men. Take a pound of almonds and blanch them, and beat them in a mortar very fine. Then take the brains of a capon and beat with it, then put into it a little cream, and make it to draw through a strainer. Then set it on the fire in a dish, and season it with rose water and sugar, and stir it.'

BAKED MALLARD

Thomas Dawson's *The good Huswifes Handmaide for the Kitchin*, 1594

'To bake a Mallard. First truss them, and parboil them, and put them into the coffin. Then season them with pepper and salt, and 4 or 5 onions peeled and sliced, and put them altogether, with a good piece of sweet butter unto the mallard. Let them bake 2 hours, and when they are baked, put in half a goblet of verjuice for every mallard, and so serve them.'

BAKED WILD DUCKS

Thomas Dawson's *The good Huswifes Handmaide for the Kitchin*, 1594

'To bake wild Ducks. Dress them fair, & parboil them, then season them with pepper & salt. Add a few whole cloves amongst them, and onions minced small, and sweet butter, verjuice, and a little sugar.'

CAPON OR ANY THING IN WHITE BROTH

Thomas Dawson's *The good Huswifes Handmaide for the Kitchin*, 1594

'To boil a Capon in white broth. Boil your capon in fair liquor, and cover it to keep it white, but you must boil no other meat with it. Take the best of the broth, and as much verjuice as of the broth, if your verjuice is not too sour. Then add whole mace, whole pepper and a good handful of endive, lettuce or borage, whichever of them you want, and small raisins, dates, marrow of marrow bones, a little stick of cinnamon and the peel of an orange. Then put in a good piece of sugar* and boil them well together. Then take 2 or 3 yolks of eggs sodden, and strain them and thicken it withall, and boil your prunes by themselves, and lay upon your capon. Pour your broth upon your Capon. Thus may you boil anything in white broth.'

*Sugar was sold in cones, of which one carved a slice, or grated.

CAPONS STEWED – HERBED CHICKEN IN SPICED WINE SAUCE

Gentyll Manly Cokere, MS Pepys 1047, *c.* 1490

'Capons stewed. Take parsley, hyssop, sage, rosemary and thyme. Break it between thy hands and stoppe [stuff] thy capons therewith, and colour them with saffron. And put them in an earthenware pot or else in brass but earthenware is better. And lay splentys [splinters? plenty?] underneath and all about the sides so that the capons touch not the sides or the bottom, and cast the same herbs into the pot among the capons. And put a quart or a pint of the best wine that thou can get and no other liquor. And set aside thereupon that will fill within the brim. And make batter of white of eggs & flour. And put between the brim a paper leaf or else loincloth, that the batter may cover it surely, so that no air comes out.

Ensure the batter is thick. And set thy pot on a charcoal fire to the mid side & see that the lid does not rise with the heat, let it stew easily and long. And when thou supposes it is enough cooked, take it from the fire. If it be a pot of earthenware, set it upon a wisp of straw so that it touches not the cold ground. And when the heat is well drawn and passed over, take off the lid. And take oute thy capons with a stick and lay them in another vessel and make a syrup of wine. And mince dates and cannela, drawn with the same wine. Add thereto currants, sugar, saffron and salt. Boil it a little and cast on powder of ginger with a little of the same wine. Pour the syrup over capons. And serve them forth with a rib of beef, ever more a capon on a dish.'

TO BOYLE QUAILES
Thomas Dawson's *The Good Huswifes Jewell*, 1596

'To boyle Quailes. First, put them into a pot with sweet broth, and set them on the fire. Then take a carrot root, and cut him in pieces, and put into the pot. Then take parsley with sweet herbs, and chop them a little, and put them into the pot. Then take cinnamon, ginger, nutmegs and pepper, and put in a little verjuice, and so season with salt. Serve them upon sops, and garnish them with fruit.'

BOILED CHICKENS AFTER THE FRENCH FASHION
Thomas Dawson's *The good Huswifes Handmaide for the Kitchin*, 1594

'To boil Chickens after the French fashion. Quarter the Chickens in four pieces: then take after the rate of a pint of wine for two Chickens. Then take thyme & parsley as small minced as ye can, and four or five Dates, with the yolks of four hard Eggs, and let this boil together, and when you will season your pot, put in salt, cinnamon and ginger, and serve it forth.'

BLAME MANGLE – CHICKEN BLANCMANGE (1)
Thomas Dawson's *The Good Huswifes Jewell*, 1596
'To make blame mangle. Take all the brain of a capon and stamp it in a mortar fine, and blanched almonds, and sometimes put to them rosewater, and season it with powder of cinnamon, ginger and sugar, and so serve it.'

BLEWE MANGER – CHICKEN BLANCMANGE (2)
A Proper New Booke of Cookery, 1545 and 1575
'To make blewe manger. Take a capon and cut out the brawn of him alive, and parboil the brawn till the flesh comes from the bone. Then fry him as dry as you can, in a fair cloth. Then take a pair of cards and card him as small as is possible, and then take a pottle of milk and a pottle of cream, and half a pound of rye flour, and your carded brawn of the capon, and put all into a pan. And stir it all together, and set it upon the fire. When it begins to boil, add thereto half a pound of beaten sugar, and a saucerful of rose water. And so let it boil till it be very thick. Then put it into a charger till it be cold, and then ye may slice it as you do leach, and so serve it.'

BLAMINGER – CHICKEN BLANCMANGE (3)
Thomas Dawson's *The good Huswifes Handmaide for the Kitchin*, 1594
'To make Blaminger. Take a Capon, boil him in fair water very tender. Then take the brawn of him & chop it small. Then take almonds, and blanch them, and beat

them small, and then put in your chopped capon and beat them together very small. Then a quart of cream and the whites of 10 eggs, & the crumb of a fine Manchet, and your mixture, and mingle them all together. Then strain them, and when it is strained put in a good quantity of sugar, and a little salt. Then take a fair pot, and put your stuff in it, and set it to the fire, stir it, and boil it as thick as an applemuse [see later recipe]. When you have boiled it, lay it in a fair platter till it be cold. Then strain it again with a little rosewater, and when you serve it, cast sugar upon it, & dish it in three parts.'

MAUNGER BLAUNCHE – CHICKEN BLANCMANGE (4)

Thomas Dawson's *The good Huswifes Handmaide for the Kitchin*, 1594

'To make Maunger Blaunche. Take half a pound of rice very clean picked and washed, then beat it very fine, and sieve it through a fine sieve, and put the finest of it in a quart of morning's milk, & strain it through a strainer. Put it in a fair pot, and set it on the fire, but it must be but a soft fire, & still stir it with a broad stick. And when it is a little thick take it from the fire, and take the brawn of a very tender capon, and pull it in as small pieces as ye can. The capon must be sodden in fair water, and the brawn of it must be pulled as small as a horse hair with your fingers. And put it into the milk which is but half thickened, and then put in as much sugar, as ye think will make it sweet. Add in a dozen spoonfuls of good rosewater, and set it on the fire again, and stir it well. And in the stirring, all to beat it with your stick, from the one side of the pan to the other. And when it is as thick as pap, take it from the fire, and put it in a fair platter, and when it is cold, lay three slices in a dish, and cast a little sugar on it, and so serve it.'

PIGEONS IN BLACK BROATH WITH FRUIT
Thomas Dawson's *The Good Huswifes Jewell*, 1596
'To boyle Pigeons in blacke broath. First roast them a little, then put them into an earthenware pot, with a little quantity of sweet broth. Then take onions, and slice them, and set them on the charcoals with some butter to take away the scent of them. Add them into the pigeons, and layer it with a toast of bread, drawn with vinegar. Then put some sweet herbs half cut, and cinnamon and ginger and gross pepper, and let them boil. And season them with salt, serve them upon sops, and garnish them with fruit.'

CAPON STEWED IN WHITE BROTH
Thomas Dawson's *The good Huswifes Handmaide for the Kitchin*, 1594
'To stew a capon in white broth. Take marrow bones with the capon, and seethe them in fair water. Add a few maces, and three races [roots] of ginger minced, and salt. When the Capon is almost sodden, put in a good quantity of lettuce, and let them seethe a while. Then serve in the capon upon sops, and the herbs upon it.'

PEACOCK WITH GINGER SAUCE
Gentyll Manly Cokere, MS Pepys 1047, *c.* 1490
'A peacock. Cut him in neck and scald him. Cut off the feet & head. Cast him on a spit. Bake him well. The sauce is ginger.'

CHICKEN AND GOOSEBERRY STEW

Thomas Dawson's *The good Huswifes Handmaide for the Kitchin*, 1594

'To stew Chickens. Take the best of your mutton broth, and put thereto a little whole pepper, and a little whole mace, parsley and thyme, and boil them. Then put in half a dish of sweet butter, verjuice, and a piece of sugar. Then take a good quantity of gooseberries, and boil them, by themselves in a little broth, and pour them upon your chickens. Put into your broth a spoonful of yeast.'

CAPON IN LEMMONS – CHICKEN IN LEMON SAUCE

A. W.'s *A Book of Cookrye*, 1584 and 1591

'To stue a Capon in Lemmons. Slice your Lemons and put them in a platter, and add to them white wine and rosewater and sugar, and so boil them till they be tender. Then take the best of the broth wherein your capon is boiled, and put thereto whole mace, whole pepper & redcurrants, barberries, a little thyme, & good store of marrow. Let them boil well together till the broth be almost boiled away that you have no more then will wet your sops. Then pour your lemons upon your capon, & season your broth with verjuice and sugar, and put it upon your capon also.'

CAPON STEWED IN LEMONS

Thomas Dawson's *The good Huswifes Handmaide for the Kitchin*, 1594

'To stew a Capon in Lemons. Take and slice your lemons, & put them in a platter, and add to them white wine, rosewater, and sugar, and so boil them and sugar till they be tender.

Then take the best of the broth wherein your capon is boiled. Add thereto whole mace, whole pepper, and redcurrants, barberries, a little thyme and good store of marrow. Let them boil well together, till the broth be almost boiled away, that you have no more than will wet your sops. Then pour your lemons upon your capon, and season your broth with verjuice and sugar, and put it also upon your capon.'

[Even in the fifteenth century, cooks were 'borrowing' each other's recipes – this is a copy of the recipe above.]

CAPON WITH ORANGES OR LEMONS

Thomas Dawson's *The good Huswifes Handmaide for the Kitchin*, 1594

'To boil a Capon with Oranges or Lemons. Take your capon and boil him tender, and take a little of the broth when it is boiled, and put it into a pipkin, with mace and sugar a good deal. Pare 3 oranges and peel them, and put them in your pipkin, and boil them a little among your broth, and thicken it with wine and yolks of eggs, and sugar a good deal, and salt but a little, and set your broth no more on the fire, for quailing, and serve it in without sippets.'

BAKED CHICKENS

Thomas Dawson's *The Second part of The Good Huswifes Jewell*, 1597

'To bake chickens. First season them with cloves & mace, pepper and salt, and put to them currants and barberries, and slit an apple and cast cinnamon and sugar upon the apple, and lay it in the bottom. To it add a dish of butter, and when it is almost enough baked, put a little sugar, verjuice and oranges.'

BOYLED CAPON OR RABBIT IN WHITE BROTH – SWEET AND SOUR ALMOND CHICKEN
Sir Hugh Plat's *Delightes for Ladies*, 1602
'To boyle a Capon in white broth. Boil your capon by itself in fair water, then take a ladleful or two of mutton broth and a little white wine, a little whole mace, a bundle of sweet herbs, a little marrow. Thicken it with almonds, season it with sugar, and a little verjuice, boil a few currants by themselves, and a date quartered, lest you discolour your broth. Put it on the breast of your capon, chicken or rabbit. If you have no almonds, thicken it with cream, or with yolks of eggs. Garnish your dishes on the sides with a lemon sliced & sugar.'

BOILED TEAL
Thomas Dawson's *The Good Huswifes Jewell*, 1596
'To boile teales. Take sweet broth [often flavoured with cinnamon and ginger] and onions, and shred them, and spinach, and put in butter and pepper. And then layer it with toasts of bread, with a little verjuice and so serve it on sops.'

CHICKEN AND MARROW IN WHITE BROTH
A Proper New Booke of Cookery, 1545 and 1575
'To stew Capon in whitebroth. Take 4 or 5 beef bones to make your broth. Then take them out when they are sodden, & strain the broth into another pot. Then put in your capons whole with rosemary, & put them into the pot and let them stew. And after they have boiled a while, put in whole mace bound in a white cloth, and a handful or two of whole parsley, and whole prunes, & let them boil well. And at the taking up, add a litle verjuice & salt,

& so strew them upon sops, and the marrowbones about, and the marrow laid whole about them, and so serve them forth.'

MORTIRS OF FOWL

Thomas Dawson's *The Second part of The Good Huswifes Jewell*, 1597

'To make Mortirs of a Capon, Hen, or pullet. Take a well fleshed capon, hen, or pullet, scald and dress him. Then put him into a pot of fair water, and there let it seethe till it be tender. Then take it and pull all the flesh from his bones, and beat it in a stone mortar, and when you think it half beaten, put some of the same liquor into it. Then beat it till it be fine, then take it out and strain it with a little rosewater out of a strainer into a dish. Then take it and set it on a chafingdish of charcoal, with a little sugar added to it, and so stir it with your knife. Lay it in a fair dish in three long rows. Then take blanch powder made of cinnamon and sugar, and cast upon it and so serve it forth.'

COLLUCE – A HEALTH DRINK

Thomas Dawson's *The Second part of The Good Huswifes Jewell*, 1597

'To make a colluce. Take all the bones and legs of the aforesaid capon, hen or pullet, and beat them fine in a stone mortar, adding to it half a pint or more of the same liquor that it was sodden in. Then strain it, and add to it a little sugar, then put it into a stone vessel, and so drink it warm first and last.'

CHEKYNS FARSED – ROAST HERB-STUFFED CHICKEN

Gentyll Manly Cokere, MS Pepys 1047, *c.* 1490

'Checkyns farsed. Break the skin at the neck behind, and blow him that the skin may arise from the flesh. Draw them, wash them clean and chop off the heads. Take the lean of fat pork boiled, and hacked small, with raw yolks of eggs and hard yolks minced small and currants and other powders & herbs parboiled and hewed small. And add in saffron and salt. Do together all these and stuff thy chickens therewith between the flesh and the skin. Plunge them in hot broth and then make them smooth with thy hands that the mixture lays even under the skin. Then parboil them a little, then roast them. And serve them forth.'

THE BOYLING OF A CAPON

Thomas Dawson's *The Good Huswifes Jewell*, 1596

'The boyling of a capon. Seethe [boil] the capon itself in water and salt and nothing else, and to make the broth. Viz. Take strong broth made with beef or mutton broth, so that it be strong broth, and put into it rosemary, parsley & thyme, with 3 leaves of sage. This let seethe in it a good while, and then put into it small raisons and a few whole mace. A quarter of an hour before it be ready to be taken from the fire, have ready cooked 4 or 5 eggs boiled hard, take nothing out but the yolks. Strain the eggs with a little of the same broth and verjuice, have a little marrow cut in small pieces, and if that time of year do serve, take the best of lettuce, cutting off the tops to the white and best, and take a few prunes with two or three dates. Thus let it seethe a quarter of an hour or more, and when it is ready to take up, have your dish with sops ready, and the water well strained out of the capon. Then season the broth with a little pepper. Then take it and dish it and scrape upon it a little sugar, laying the prunes round about the dish side.'

GUSSET – CHICKEN POTAGE
A Proper New Booke of Cookery, 1545 and 1575
'For Gusset, that may be another potage. Take the broth of the same capons, and put it in a faire chafer. Then take a dozen or 16 eggs, and stir them all together white and all, then grate a farthing white loaf [this could weigh around five pounds, the price regulated by law] as small as ye can, and mince it with the eggs altogether. And add thereto salt, and a good quantity of saffron, and add into your eggs. Put into your broth thyme, savoury, marjoram, and parsley small chopped. And when ye are ready to your dinner, set the chafer upon the fire with the broth, and let it boil a little, and put in your eggs, and stir it up well for quailing the less. The less boiling it hath, the more tender it will be, and then serve it forth two or three slices upon a dish.'

CHICKENS UPON SOPPES
A Proper New Booke of Cookery, 1545 and 1575
'Chickens upon soppes. Take sorell sauce a good quantity, and put in cinnamon and sugar, and let it boil, and pour it upon the sops, and then lay on the chickens.'

FRIED CHICKINS BEFORE KENTUCKY WAS INVENTED*
Thomas Dawson's *The Good Huswifes Jewell*, 1596
'To frie Chickins. Take your chickens and let them boil in very good sweet broth a pretty while. Take the chickens

out, and quarter them out in pieces, and then put them into a frying pan with sweet butter. Let them stew in the pan, but you must not let them be brown with frying. Then put the butter out of the pan. Then take a little sweet broth, and as much verjuice, and the yolks of 2 eggs, and beat them together, and put in a little nutmeg, cinnamon, ginger and pepper into the sauce. Then add them all into the pan with the chicken pieces, and stir them together in the pan, and put them into a dish, and serve them up.'

*The 'Bluegrass State', officially the 'Commonwealth of Kentucky', is only one of four US states designated as a commonwealth, along with Virginia, Pennsylvania and Massachusetts. Kentucky was the fifteenth state to join the Union, in 1792.

HOT COFFINS OF CHICKIN AND FRUIT
A Proper New Booke of Cookery, 1545 and 1575
'To bake Chickins in like paste. Take your chickens & season them with a litle ginger & salt, and so put them into your coffin. Add in them barberries, grapes or goseberries, & half a dish of butter, so close them up. Set them in the oven, & when they are baked, take the yolks of 6 eggs, and a dishful of verjuice, and draw them through a strainer. Set them upon a chafingedish, then draw your baked chickens, and add thereto this aforesaid eggs and verjuice and thus serve them hot.'

BOILED CHICKINS WITH LEMMAN
Thomas Dawson's *The Good Huswifes Jewell*, 1596
'To boile Chickins. Strain your broth into a pipkin, & put in your chickens, and skim them as clean as you can. Add a piece of butter, and a good deal of sorrel, and so

let them boil. Add in all manner of spices, and a little verjuice and a few barberries. And cut a lemon in pieces, and scrape a little sugar upon them, and lay them upon the chickens when you serve them up, and lay sops upon the dish.'

BAKED CHICKEN AND DAMSONS
Thomas Dawson's *The good Huswifes Handmaide for the Kitchin*, 1594
'To bake Chickens with Damsons. Take your chickens, draw them and wash them, then break their bones, and lay them in a platter. Then take 4 handfuls of fine flour, and lay it on a fair board. Put thereto 12 yolks of eggs, a dish of butter, and a little saffron. Mingle them altogether, & make your paste therewith. Then make 6 coffins, and put in every coffin a lump of butter of the bigness of a walnut. Then season your 6 coffins with one spoonful of cloves and mace, 2 spoonfuls of cinnamon, and one of Sugar, and a spoonful of Salt. Then put your Chickens into your pies. Then take damsons and pare away the outward peel of them. Add 20 in every of your pies, round about your chicken, then put into every of your coffins, a handful of currants. Then close them up, and put them into the oven, then let them be there three quarters of an hour.'

BAKED TURKIE
Thomas Dawson's *The good Huswifes Handmaide for the Kitchin*, 1594
'To bake a Turkie. Take and cleave your turkey on the back, and bruise all the bones. Then season it with salt, and pepper gross beaten, and put into it good store of butter: he must have 5 hours baking.'

10. Turkeys only came to prominence following their arrival from America in 1519. For centuries, swan or goose remained the traditional meat on Christmas Day.

BAKED FESANT

Thomas Dawson's *The good Huswifes Handmaide for the Kitchin*, 1594

'To bake a Fesant. Truss him like a hen, and parboil him, then set him with cloves, then take a little verjuice and saffron, and colour it with a feather. And take salt, mace and ginger to season it, and so put it in the pastry, and bake it till it be half enough. Then put in a little verjuice and the yolk of an egg beaten together. Then bake it till it be enough.'

CHICKEN IN WHITE BROTH WITH ALMONDS

Thomas Dawson's *The Good Huswifes Jewell*, 1596

'To boile a capon in white broth with almondes. Take your capon with marrowbones and set them on the fire, and when they be clean skimmed, take the fattest of the broth. Put it in a little pot with a good deal of marrow, prunes, raisons, whole dates, maces, & a pint of white wine. Then blanch your almonds and strain them. With them thicken your pot & let it seethe a good while and when it is enough serve it upon sops with your capon.'

BAKED PHEASANT OR CAPON
John Partridge's *The Treasurie of commodious Conceits*, 1573
'To bake a Fesant, or Capon in steede of a Fesant. Dress your capon like a pheasant trussed, parboiled a little & larded with sweet lard. Put him into the coffin, cast thereon a little pepper and salt. Add thereto half a dish of sweet butter, let it bake for the space of 3 hours, & when it is cold serve it forth for a pheasant. And thus bake a pheasant.'

BAKED CAPON INSTEAD OF A PHEASANT
Thomas Dawson's *The good Huswifes Handmaide for the Kitchin*, 1594
'To bake a Capon in steed of Feasant. Cut off his legs and his wings, and after the manner of a pheasant truss him short. Then parboil him a little, and lard him with sweet lard. And so put him into the coffin, and take a little pepper and salt and cast about him. And take a good half dish of butter and put into the coffin, so let him bake the space of 4 hours and serve it forth cold instead of pheasant. So likewise bake a pheasant.'
[This is, again, a later copy of the recipe above.]

BAKED CRANE OR BUSTARD
Thomas Dawson's *The good Huswifes Handmaide for the Kitchin*, 1594

'To bake a Crane or a Bustard. Parboil him a little, then lard him with sweet [unsalted] lard, and put him in the coffin. Take pepper and salt a good quantity, and season them together, and cast upon it. Then take butter, and put in the coffin, let it bake 3 hours.'

[Birds like bittern, stork, crane, bustard and egret were far more common in Tudor times.]

PIGEON PIES
A Proper New Booke of Cookery, 1545 and 1575

'To bake pigeons in short paste as you make to your baken Apples. Season your pigeons with pepper, saffron, cloves and mace, with verjuice and salt. Then put them into your paste, and so close them up, and bake them. They will bake in half an hour, then take them forth, and if ye think them dry, take a little verjuice and butter, and add to them, and so serve them.'

ORANGE AND LEMON BOILED CHICKEN
Thomas Dawson's *The Good Huswifes Jewell*, 1596

'To boile a Capon with Oranges and Lemmons. Take oranges or lemons peeled, and cut them the long way, and if you can keep your cloves whole, and put them into your best broth of mutton or capon with prunes or currants and 3 or 4 dates. When these have been well sodden add whole pepper, great mace, a good piece of sugar, some rosewater, and either white or claret wine, and let all these seethe together awhile, & so serve it upon sops with your capon.'

BOILED MALLARD WITH CABBAGE

Thomas Dawson's *The good Huswifes Handmaide for the Kitchin*, 1594

'To boil a Mallard with Cabage. Take the cabbage and pick them clean, and wash and parboil in fair water. Then put in a colander, and let the water run from the cabbage, then put them in a fair pot, and as much beef broth as will cover them. Add the marrow of 3 marrowbones whole. Then take a mallard, and with your knife give him a lance along upon each side of the breast. Then take him off, and put him into your cabbage, and his dripping with him, for he must be roasted half enough, and his dripping saved, and so let them stew the space of one hour. Then put in some pepper and a little salt, & serve in your mallard upon sops, and the cabbage about him, with the uppermost of the broth.'

BOILED MALLARD WITH ONIONS

Thomas Dawson's *The good Huswifes Handmaide for the Kitchin*, 1594

'To boil a Mallard with Onions. Take a mallard, roast him half enough, and save the dripping. Then put him into a fair pot, and his gravy with him, and put into his belly 6 or 7 whole onions, and a spoonful of whole pepper, and as much abroad in your pot. Add to it as much mutton broth or beef broth as will cover the mallard, and half a dish of sweet butter, two spoonfuls of verjuice, and let them boil the space of an hour. Then add in some salt, and take off the pot, and lay the mallard upon sops, and the onions about him, and pour the uppermost of the broth upon them.'

BOILED CHICKENS AND MUTTON AFTER THE DUTCH FASHION

Thomas Dawson's *The Second part of The Good Huswifes Jewell*, 1597

'To boil chickens and mutton after the Dutch fashion. First take chickens and mutton, and boil them in water a good while, and let a good deal of the water be boiled away. Then take out the mutton and chickens and the broth. Make white broth, put in thereto cinnamon and ginger, sugar and a little pepper, and a little verjuice, and a little flour to thicken it, and a little saffron, take rosemary, thyme, marjoram and pennyroyal, and hyssop, and half a dish of butter, with a little salt, the liquor must be cold before the chickens be put in.'

CHICKEN, SPINACH AND LETTICE

Thomas Dawson's *The Second part of The Good Huswifes Jewell*, 1597

'To boil chickens with Spinach and Lettice. Take a platter of spinach and lettuce, and wash them clean, and when the pot is skimmed, then put them in with a dish of butter, and a branch of rosemary with a little verjuice, being seasoned with salt and ginger beaten.'

[Dawson does not mention chicken, so one presumes that boiled chicken is placed upon the greens.]

BAKED CAPON WITH EGG YOLKS

John Partridge's *The Treasurie of commodious Conceits*, 1573

'To bake a Capon with yolkes of Egges. When the capon is made ready, truss him in the coffin. Then take 8 yolks of eggs sodden hard, & prick into every of them 5 cloves, & put the yolks into the coffin with the capon. Then take a quantity of ginger and salt, and cast it on the capon, and let it bake 3 hours. Then take 2 raw yolks of eggs beaten into a goblet of verjuice, with a good quantity of sugar sodden together, put it into ye coffin and so serve it.'

CAPON IN SPINNAGE SIRROP
Thomas Dawson's *The Good Huswifes Jewell*, 1596
'To boile a capon with a sirrop. Boil your capon in sweet broth, and put in gross pepper and whole mace into the capon's belly. Make your syrup with spinach, white wine, currants, sugar, cinnamon and ginger, and sweet butter, and so let them boil. When your capon is ready to serve put the syrup on the capon, and boil your spinach before you make your syrup.'

BOILED CHICKEN
Thomas Dawson's *The good Huswifes Handmaide for the Kitchin*, 1594
'To boil Chickens or Capons. First boil them in fair water till they be tender. Then take bread and steep it in the broth of them, and with the yolks of 4 or 5 eggs, and verjuice or white wine. Strain it, and therewith season your broth and your capon in it. Then take butter, parsley, and other small herbs, and chop them into it. And so serve them forth upon sops of bread.'

BOILED CHICKENS WITH A CAWDEL
Thomas Dawson's *The good Huswifes Handmaide for the Kitchin*, 1594
'To boil Chickens with a Cawdel.' Take your chickens when they are fair scalded, and trussed and stuffed with

parsley in their bellies. Put them in a pot with fair water and a little salt. Put to them 20 Prunes, half a handful of currants and raisins, and let them boil altogether till your chickens be tender. Then take 6 yolks, and a pint of Vinegar, and strain them together, and put thereto a quartern [a fourth part measure] of sugar, or as ye think fit, and so let it boil. But ye must still stir it, else it will curdle. And when it boils, take it from the fire. Then take your chickens, and put them in a colander, that the broth may go clean away, and so put your chickens and the fruit into the cawdel. And make sops, and lay on your chickens and the fruit, and pour on the cawdel.'

[*Cawdel* is the Welsh for a hotchpotch or mess, and 'coddle' probably derives from it.].

BAKED CHICKINS IN A CAWDLE

Thomas Dawson's *The Good Huswifes Jewell*, 1596

'To bake Chickins in a Cawdle. Season them with salt and pepper, and put in butter, and so let them bake. When they be baked, boil a few barberries and prunes and currants and take a little white wine or verjuice. Let it boil and add in a little sugar, and set it on the fire a little, and strain in 2 or 3 yolks of eggs into the wine. And when you take the dish off the fire, put the prunes and currants and barberries into the dish. Then put them in altogether into the pie of chickens.'

HOW TO SEETHE HENNES AND CAPONS IN WINTER IN WHITE BROTH

Thomas Dawson's *The good Huswifes Handmaide for the Kitchin*, 1594

'How to seethe Hennes and Capons [a capon is a large, castrated cockerel] in Winter in white broth. Take a neck of mutton and a marrow bone, and let them boil with the hens together. Then take carrot roots and put them into the pot, and then strain a little bread to thicken the pot withall and not too thick. Season it with pepper and verjuice, and then cover them close, and then let them boil together. Then cut sops and add the broth and the marrow above, and so serve them.'

BOILED, SPICED CAPON AND MUTTON

Thomas Dawson's *The Second part of The Good Huswifes Jewell*, 1597

'To boil a Capon. Let your capon be fair scalded and short trussed, and put into a fair pot of water with a marrowbone or two, & a rack of mutton cut together in 3 or 4 pieces. Let them boil together till they be half boiled. Then take out a ladleful or two of the best of the broth, and put it into a fair earthenware pot & add thereto a pint of white wine or of claret, and cut 12 or 14 dates longways & a handful of small raisins, a handful of thyme, rosemary and hyssop bound together, and so let these parcels boil by themselves. And when your capon is enough cooked, lay it in a fair platter upon sops of white bread, and your mutton by him also, then take out the marrow from the bones whole, and lay it upon the capon. Then take your made broth & lay it upon your capon & mutton, and so serve it forth. Your latter broth must be seasoned with cinnamon, cloves and mace, and salt and mace beaten also.'

BALDRICK'S BOYLED DUCK WITH TURNEPS

Thomas Dawson's *The Good Huswifes Jewell*, 1596

'To boyle a Ducke with Turneps. Take her first, and put her into a pot with stewed broth. Then take parsley, and sweet herbs, and chop them. Parboil the roots very well in another pot, then add unto them sweet butter, cinnamon, ginger, gross pepper and whole mace, and so season it with salt, and serve it upon sops.'

CHICKENS SEETHED IN LETTICE
Thomas Dawson's *The good Huswifes Handmaide for the Kitchin*, 1594
'To seethe Chickens in Lettice. Take a neck of mutton with a marrow bone, and so let it seethe, and skim it clean, and let it boil well together. When it is enough cooked, then take out some of it, and strain it, and put in your chickens. Then take a good many lettuces, and wash them clean and put them in. Then take a little white bread and strain it, and put it into the pot to thicken it withall. Then put a little whole mace to season it, with pepper and verjuice, and a little sugar, and cut sops, and lay them on, and put on the marrow and so serve them.'

HOW TO BOIL CHICKENS [MUTTON, PIGEONS OR RABBITS] WITH HERBS
Thomas Dawson's *The good Huswifes Handmaide for the Kitchin*, 1594
'How to boil chickens with herbs. Take your chickens and scald them, and truss the wings on, and put their feet under the wings of your chickens, and set them on in a little pot and skim them fair. When they have boiled, put in spinach or lettuce a good deal, and rosemary, sweet butter, verjuice, salt, and a little sugar, and strained bread with a little wine, and cut sippets and serve it out. So may you boil mutton, or pigeons or rabbit.'

CAPON WITH ORANGES

Thomas Dawson's *The Second part of The Good Huswifes Jewell*, 1597

'To boil a capon with Oranges. Take your capon & set him on the fire as before with marrow bones & mutton. When you have skimmed the pot well, put thereto the value of a farthing loaf, and let it boil till it be half boiled, then take 2 or 3 ladlefuls of ye same broth and put it into an earthenware pot, with a pint of the wine aforesaid, and peel 6 or 8 oranges and slice them thin. Put them into the same broth with 4 pennyworth in sugar or more, and a handful of parsley, thyme, and rosemary together tied, and season it with whole mace, cloves & sticks of cinnamon with two nutmeg, beaten small and so serve it.'

4

Seafood and Freshwater Dishes

FISH DAY SALADS

Thomas Dawson's *The Second part of The Good Huswifes Jewell*, 1597

Sallets for fish daies.

First a sallet of green fine herbs, putting Perriwincles among them with oyle and vineger.

Olives and Capers in one dish, with vineger and oyle.

White Endive in a dish with periwincles upon it, and oyle and vineger.

Carret rootes being minced, and then made in the dish, after the proportion of a Flowerdeluce [fleur-de-lis lily], then picke Shrimps and lay upon it with oyle and vineger.

Onions in flakes laid round about the dishe, with minced carrets laid in the middle of the dish, with boild Hippes in five partes like an Oken leafe, made and garnished with tawney long cut with oil and vineger.

Alexander buds cut long waies, garnished with welkes.

Skirret [like carrot or parsnip] rootes cut long waies in a dish with tawney long cutte, vineger and Oyle.

Salmon cut long waies, with slices of onions laid upon it, and upon that to cast violets, oyle and vineger.

Take pickelde herring cut long waies and lay them in rundles with onions and parsely chopped, and other herringes the bones being taken out to bee chopped together and laide in the roundles with a long peece laide betwixt the rundles like the proportion of a snake, garnished with Tawney long cut, with vineger and oile. Take pickelde Herrings and cut them long waies, and so lay them in a dish, and serve them with oyle and vineger.'

'FULL WALLOP' SEETHED SHRIMPS

A. W.'s *A Book of Cookrye*, 1584 and 1591

'How to seeth Shrimps. Take half water and half beer or ale, and some salt good and savoury. Set it on the fire and faire skim it, and when it seethes [boils] a full wallop*, put in your shrimps faire washed, and seethe them with a quick fire. Scum them very clean, and let them have but two walmes [coming to the boil], then take them up with a skimmer, and lay them upon a fair white cloth, and sprinkle a little white salt upon them.'

*The series of noisy bubbling motions made by water, when rapidly boiling, or approaching boiling point, e.g. in a phrase 'to boil [seethe] a wallop', a full wallop, to boil with a rapid noisy bubbling, to 'gallop'.

BOILED COCKLES

Thomas Dawson's *The Second part of The Good Huswifes Jewell*, 1597

'To boil cockles. Take water, vinegar, pepper, and beer, and put the cockles in it, then let them seethe a good while, & serve them broth and all. You may seethe them in nothing but in water and salt if you will.'

11. Billingsgate Market, London, depicted in 1598. Billingsgate was both a specialist fish market and a place for buying other foodstuffs brought to London along the Thames.

TO BOILE MUSKLES
Thomas Dawson's *The Good Huswifes Jewell*, 1596
'To boile Muskles. Take water and yeast, and a good dish of butter, and onions chopped, and a little pepper. When it hath boiled a little while, then see that your mussels be clean washed, then put them into the broth shells and all, and when they be boiled well, then serve them broth and all.'

SEETHING MUSCLES
Thomas Dawson's *The Second part of The Good Huswifes Jewell*, 1597
'To seethe Muscles. Take butter and vinegar a good deal, parsley chopped small and pepper, then set it on the fire, and let it boil a while, then see the mussels be clean washed, and put them in the broth shells and all, and when they be boiled a while, serve them shells and all.'
[While the best place for *moules frites* (mussels and chips) is Belgium, the following modern redaction tastes excellent: Take 4 pounds of mussels; ½ cup red wine vinegar; 2 garlic

cloves, minced; 2 tbsp butter; ½ cup chopped parsley; ¾ tsp salt; ¼ tsp freshly ground black pepper. Place the mussels in cold water and scrub them clean, 'bearding' them by taking off the tuft of fibres projecting from the shell. However, many farm-raised mussels lack this beard. Discard any mussels which are broken or do not close when touched. Place 1 cup of water and all ingredients except the mussels into a large pot, cover, and bring to a boil over high heat. Add the mussels and reduce the heat so that the mussels cook at a simmer. Cook, shaking the pot occasionally, for 10 minutes or until all of the mussels have opened fully. Never overcook, as the mussels become chewy. Never attempt to open and eat any mussels that have not opened. Pour the mussels with their broth into bowls, setting another empty bowl on the table for discarded shells. Mop up the broth with fresh crusty bread.]

DRESSED CRABBE
A Proper New Booke of Cookery, 1545 and 1575
'To dresse a Crabbe. First take away all the legs and the heads & then take all the fish out of the shell, and make the shell as clean as ye can. Put the meat into a dish, & butter it upon a chafingdish of charcoal, and put thereto cinnamon and sugar, and a little vinegar. When ye have chafed it, and seasoned it, then put the meat into the shell again, and bruise the heads, & set them upon the dish side, and serve it.'

CRABMEAT DRESSED IN SHELL
Gentyll Manly Cokere, MS Pepys 1047, *c.* 1490
'To dyght a crabe. Take out all in the crab and lay it in a little vinegar. Take and add a little red wine thereto

and strain all through a strainer. Take powder of ginger, cinnamon, and sugar and mix all together. And put him in the shell. And set it on the fire till he boils, and when it is boiled take it off. Cast powder of cinnamon and sugar upon and serve it forth.'

BAKED OR BROILED LOBSTER WITH VINEGAR AS A DIP
Gentyll Manly Cokere, MS Pepys 1047, *c.* 1490
'A Lopstere. A lobster shall be baked in an oven or under a pan by the fireside and then eat him with vinegar.'

OYSTER CHEWETS
The Good Hous-wiues Treasurie, 1588
'To make Oister Chewets. Take a peck [2 gallons] of oysters & wash them clean, then shell them and wash them faire in a colander. When they be sodden, strain the water from them, and chop them as small as pie meat. Then season them with pepper, half a pennyworth of cloves and mace, half a pennyworth of cinnamon and ginger, and a pennyworth of sugar, a little saffron & salt, then take a handful of small raisins and 6 dates minced small. Mingle them all together, then make your pastry with one pennyworth of fine flour, 10 yolks of eggs, a half pennyworth of butter with a little saffron and boiling water. Then raise up your chewets and put in the bottom of every one of them a little butter, and so fill them with your stuff. Then cast prunes, dates, and small raisins upon them, and being closed, bake them. Let not your oven be too hot for they will have but little baking. Then draw them out, and put into every one of them two spoonfuls of verjuice and butter, and so serve them.'

STEWED OYSTERS

Thomas Dawson's *The Second part of The Good Huswifes Jewell*, 1597

'To stewe Oysters. Take your oysters, and put them either in a little skillet over the fire, or else in a platter over a chafingdish of charcoal, and so let them boil with their liquor, sweet butter, verjuice, vinegar and pepper, and of the tops of thyme a little, till they be enough cooked, and then serve them upon sops.'

TO BAKE OYSTERS SHELS AND ALL

Thomas Dawson's *The good Huswifes Handmaide for the Kitchin*, 1594

'To bake Oysters shels and all. Take the best oysters fair shelled, and the fairest & smoothest shells. Wash a good many, and to make them smooth, rub one shell against another, and when they are very clean make your pie. Then let your gravy run through a strainer of your oysters and wash your oysters very clean, and season them with pepper and salt. Then take out of the deepest shells, and put into them 3 oysters and 3 cloves, and a little piece of butter, and lay a flat shell upon that. And thus set your pie with the shells and the oysters in them till they be full, and in void places put in a piece of butter. Then close your pie, and set it into the oven and when it hath stood there half an hour draw out your pie. Then put in a saucer full of your gravy. Then put the pie into the oven again, and so let it stand one other half hour, and then serve it forth.'

STURGEON IN VINEGAR
Gentyll Manly Cokere, MS Pepys 1047, *c.* 1490
'Sturgeon. Take and lay him in water overnight. Seethe him and let him cool and lay him in vinegar or aysell [cider or wine vinegar] that sauce is kindly there to serve it forth.'
[Under British law, whales and sturgeon are 'royal fish', the property of the monarch. This particular royal prerogative dates from the time of Edward II, and in 2004 a Llanelli fisherman was investigated for landing a ten-foot sturgeon in Swansea Bay and selling it in Plymouth for £650. Sturgeon is now very rare in European waters.]

GURNARD IN ALE, PEPPER AND VINEGAR SAUCE
Gentyll Manly Cokere, MS Pepys 1047, *c.* 1490
'Gurnard. Take him and slit a little the womb and take out the guts. Seethe him in salt water and ale. The sauce is pepper and vinegar.' [A gurnard was a sea robin.]

WHITE FISH FRICASE
A. W.'s *A Book of Cookrye*, 1584 and 1591
'To make a Fricase of a good Haddock or Whiting. First seethe the fish and scum it, and pick out the bones. Take onions and chop them small then fry them in butter or oil till they be enough cooked. Put in your fish, and fry them till it be dry. That done, serve it forth with powder of ginger on it.'

BOILED FISH OF ALL KINDS
Thomas Dawson's *The Good Huswifes Jewell*, 1596
'To boile divers kindes of fishes. Bret, conger, thornback ray, plaice, fresh salmon, all these you must boil with a

little fair water and vinegar, a little salt, and bay leaves, and sauce them in vinegar, and a little of the broth that they are sodden in with a little salt, and as you see cause shift your sauce, as you do beef in brine, and also fresh sturgeon, seethe it as is aforesaid, and sauce it as ye did the other, and so ye may keep it half a year with changing of the sauce. And salt sturgeon seethe it in water & salt, and a little vinegar, and let it be cold, and serve it forth with vinegar, and a little fennel upon it, but first or ye seethe it, it must be watered.'

PIKE IN ALE AND HERBS
Gentyll Manly Cokere, MS Pepys 1047, *c.* 1490
'For to seth a pyke. Kill him in the head. Stick [it to the table] and take a handful of great salt. Rub him till the

12. A sixteenth-century Dutch print showing bream, a mackerel, two sea robins (gurnard) and lumpfish washed up on the beach. Fish were highly popular, with religion playing a big part in their prominence.

flewme go from him. Open him at the belly and take out the refete [also spelt refette, edible entrails], and take out the gall and strip all the small guts and cast them away and save the great gut. Take a fair clean pan and a quart of fair water. Take a quart of new ale and a dish full of este and take 2 handfuls of salt and cast therein. Take a little ginger and cinnamon and cast thereto rosemary, marjoram, thyme and parsley and a little savory, and break all these herbs in two. Cast in the pan. If he be not well refete [with oil proceeding from his edible organs], cast in a little suet butter but seethe it.'

MUSTARD SAUCE FOR A PIKE
Gentyll Manly Cokere, MS Pepys 1047, *c.* 1490
'To make sauce for a pyke. Take the refette of the pike and mince it small and put it in a dish and take a good mass of mustard. And put the best and fattest of the broth in a saucer and shake and add it in to the dish with the minced refette. Add a little vinegar and a little verjuice thereto, and a great quantity of cinnamon & sugar and little ginger and as ye feel iit with your mouth ye may always amend it.'

QIKESAUCE FOR BROKEFISH – FRESHWATER FISH SAUCE
A Proper New Booke of Cookery, 1545 and 1575
'A qikesauce for a pike, Breeme, perch, Roche, Carp, Eeles, Flookes, and all manner of Brokefish. Take a posy of rosemary and thyme, and bind them together, and put in also a quantity of parsley not bound. Put into the cauldron of water, salt and yeast, and the herbs, and let them boil a pretty while. Then put in the fish and a good

quantity of butter, and let them boil a good season, and you shall have good pike sauce.

For all these fishes above written, if they must be broiled, take sauce for them, butter, pepper and vinegar, and boil it upon a chafingdish, and then lay the broiled fish upon the dish. But for eels and fresh salmon nothing but pepper and vinegar over boiled. And also if you will fry them, you must take a good quantity of parsley. After the fish is fried, put the parsley into the frying pan, and let it fry in the butter, and take it up, and put it on the fried fish, and fried plaice, whiting, and such other fish except eels, fresh salmon, conger, which be never fried, but baked, broiled, roasted, or sodden.'

FRIED WHITINGS
A. W.'s *A Book of Cookrye*, 1584 and 1591

'To fry Whitings. First flay them and wash them clean and scale them. That done, lap them in flour and fry them in butter and oil. Then to serve them, mince apples or onions and fry them, then put them into a vessel with white wine, verjuice, salt, pepper, cloves & mace, and boil them together on the charcoal, and serve it upon the whitings.'

SALMON ALOES
Thomas Dawson's *The Second part of The Good Huswifes Jewell*, 1597

'To make alloes of fresh Salmon to boil or to bake. Take your Salmon and cut him small in pieces of three fingers breadth, and when you have cut so many slices as you will have, let them be of the length of a woman's hand, then take more of the salmon, as much as you think good. And mince it raw with 6 yolks of hard Eggs chopped very fine, and then 2 or 3 dishes of butter with small raisins, and so work them together with cloves, mace, pepper and salt. Then lay your minced meat in your sliced aloes, every one being rolled and pricked with a feather, fall closed. Then put your aloes into an earthenware pot, and add to it a pint of water, and another pint of Claret wine. And so let them boil till they be cooked enough, & afterward take the yolks of 3 raw eggs with a little verjuice, being strained together, and so put into the pot. Then let your aloes seethe no more afterward, but serve them upon sops of bread.'

SAMON ROSTYD IN SAUCE – GRILLED SALMON IN WINE SAUCE
Gentyll Manly Cokere, MS Pepys 1047, *c.* 1490

'Samon rostyd in sause. Cut thy salmon in round pieces and roast it on a gridiron. Take wine and powder of cinnamon and draw them through a strainer. Add thereto onions minced small. Boil it well. Take vinegar or verjuice and powder of ginger and salt. Add thereto. Lay the salmon in dishes and pour the syrup thereon and serve forth.'

PIKE FOR A BANQUET WITH AN ORANGE IN ITS MOUTH
Thomas Dawson's *The Second part of The Good Huswifes Jewell*, 1597

'To boil a pike with oranges a banquet dish. Take your pike, splet [divide] him, and seethe him alone with water, butter, & salt. Then take an earthenware pot and put into it a pint of water, and another of wine, with 2 oranges or 2 lemons if you have them. If not, then take 4 or 5 oranges, the rinds being cut away, and sliced. And so add to the liquor, with 6 dates cut longways, and season your broth with ginger, pepper and salt, and two dishes of sweet butter. Boil these together, and when you will serve it, lay your pike upon sops, casting your broth upon it. You must remember that you cut off your pike's head hard by the body & then his body to be divided, cutting every side in two or three parts, and when he is enough, set the body of the fish in order. Then take his head & set it at the foremost part of the dish, standing upright with an orange in his mouth, and so serve him.'

BREAM IN WHITE WINE
Thomas Dawson's *The Good Huswifes Jewell*, 1596
'To boile a Breame. Take white wine and put it into a pot, and let it seethe. Then take your bream and cut him in the midst, and put him in. Then take an onion and chop it small. Then take nutmegs beaten, cinnamon and ginger, whole mace, and a pound of butter, and let it boil altogether. And so season it with salt, serve it upon sops, and garnish it with fruit.'

MORTREWS OF FYSHE
Gentyll Manly Cokere, MS Pepys 1047, *c.* 1490
'To make mortrews of fyshe. Take houndfish [dogfish], haddock or cod. Boil it and pick it clean from the bones. Take away the skin and grind the liver with blanched almonds. And temper thy milk with the broth of the fresh fish and make a good milk of it. Add thereto crumbs of white bread and sugar. Set it to the fire. When it boils look it be standing. Mess [portion out]. Serve it forth. Strew on poudre blanche*.'

*Poudre blanche, white powder, was a popular sweet-and-savoury concoction probably brought back by the Crusaders – mix 3 tbsp of sugar, 1 tbsp of ground nutmeg and 1 tbsp of ground ginger.

BOILED CARP

Thomas Dawson's *The Second part of The Good Huswifes Jewell*, 1597

'To boil a Carpe. Take out the gall, cast it away, and so scald not your carp nor yet wash him, & when you do kill him let his blood fall into a platter. Divide your carp into the same blood, and cast thereon a ladleful of vinegar, then toast 3 or 4 toasts of brown bread and burn them black. Place them into a little fair water, and then immediately strain them into the liquor where your carp shall be sodden with 3 or 4 onions chopped somewhat big, with parsley chopped small. Then set your broth upon the fire, and when it begins to boil, add to your carp 2 or 3 dishes of butter, and a branch of rosemary slips, and slips of thyme. If it be too thick, add to it a little wine, and so let it boil fair and softly. Season it with whole mace, cloves and salt, and pepper, cloves and mace beaten, and so serve it.'

[Carp, like pike, is no longer a popular dish, but the advent of eastern Europeans into the UK is bringing a greater demand for both fish.]

TROUT PATÉ PIES

Thomas Dawson's *The Second part of The Good Huswifes Jewell*, 1597

'A Troute baked or minced. Take a trout and seethe him, then take out all the bones, then mince it very fine with 3 or 4 dates minced with it, seasoning it with ginger, and cinnamon, and a quantity of sugar and butter. Add all these together, working them fast. Then take your fine pastry, and cut it in three corner ways in a small bigness, of 4 or 5 coffins in a dish, then lay your stuff in them. Close them, and so bake them and in the serving of them baste the covers with a little butter, and then cast a little blaunch poudre on them, and so serve it forth.'

BAKED FISH

A. W.'s *A Book of Cookrye*, 1584 and 1591

'To bake Carp, Bream, Mullet, Pike, Trout, Roche or any other kinde of Fish. Season them with cloves and mace, and pepper and bake them with small raisins [sultanas], sweet butter and verjuice, great raisins, and some prunes.'

13. Tudor women offering freshly gutted fish to a traveller.

BAKED PORPOISE OR SEAL

Thomas Dawson's *The Second part of The Good Huswifes Jewell*, 1597

'To bake porpoise or Seale. Take your porpoise or seal, and parboil it, seasoning it with pepper and salt. And so bake it. You must take off the skin when you bake it and then serve it forth with gallentine sauce [see later recipe] in saucers.'

STEWED HERYNGS – HERRINGS IN MUSTARD ALE SAUCE (1)

Gentyll Manly Cokere, MS Pepys 1047, *c.* 1490

'For to stew heryng'. See thy heryng be well watered [rested and rinsed in fresh water] and take out the bone and take the milts and lay them in a fair dish of water. Wash both the herring and the milt together. Then take a little parsley, as much thyme, a few onions and meld all together as small as ye can make it. Then bruise all your herbs and the milt together. And take powder of pepper, a little sugar and currants, and crumbs of white bread and put all these together and stew thy herring withall. When they be stuffed, lay them on a dish and take of ale a good portion, and put thereto mustard and cast upon them great raisins. Cover them with a dish and set them on the fire and so serve them forth.'

STEWED HERRINGES (2)

Thomas Dawson's *The good Huswifes Handmaide for the Kitchin*, 1594

'To stew Herringes. Take ale, and put therein a few onions small cut, & a spoonful of mustard, great raisins and saffron. Thicken it with grated bread. If you will have

puddings in them, take the soft roes of the herrings, &
stamp them with a little thick almond milk. Add thereto
some dates or figs minced, cloves, mace, sugar, saffron,
salt, some currants, and grated bread.'

BOILED SALMON
Thomas Dawson's *The Second part of The Good Huswifes
Jewell*, 1597

'For fresh Salmon. Take your salmon and boil him in
fair water, rosemary and thyme, and in the boiling add a
quart of strong ale to it. And so let it boil till it be enough,
then take it from the fire, and let it cool. Then take your
salmon out of the pan, and put it into an earthenware
pan or wooden bowl, and there put so much broth as will
cover it. Add into the same broth a good deal of vinegar,
so that it be tart with it.'

HERRING PIES
Thomas Dawson's *The good Huswifes Handmaide for the
Kitchin*, 1594

'To make Hering pies. Take herrings and crush them in
your hands, so shall ye loose the flesh from the skin. Save
the skin as whole as ye can, and scrape off all the fish,
that none may be left thereupon. Then take a pound of
almonds, or as many as ye be disposed to make, blanch
them, and stamp them, and in the stamping of them, put
in one soft roe, and one hard roe, and 5 or 6 Dates, and a
spoonful or two of grated bread, and a pint of Muscadell
[a white wine] to grind them withall. But ye may not
grind them too fine, nor may not make them too moist
with your Muskadell, but somewhat stiff, that you may
fill the skins of your herrings. Then take rosewater, and a
little saffron, to colour the almonds withall, when ye have

ground them. Then put in 4 dates, and cut them fine, and a handful of currants, and a little sugar. Then make fine pastry, and roll it as thin as you can, and strew thereon a good deal of sugar, then put your herrings therein, and bake them.'

14. An early seventeenth-century work by Jan van de Velde showing wealthy and well-dressed ladies and gentlemen attending a vegetable market. A stall can be seen in the centre.

Of Potatoes of Virginia.

Battata Virginiana sue Virginianorum, & Pappus.
Potatoes of Virginia.

15. Potatoes from Gerarde's Herbal, 1597. Potatoes were first brought to England in the 1580s but few English people ate them, whereas sweet potatoes featured fairly prominently after their discovery. According to conservative estimates, the introduction of the potato was responsible for a quarter of the growth in Old World population and urbanisation between 1700 and 1900. Its high carbohydrate content as a staple diet for the hard-working masses, and ease of storage over winter, helped ease epidemics of starvation.

5

Vegetable Recipes

FRIED BEANS
A Proper New Booke of Cookery, 1545 and 1575
'To fry Beanes. Take your beans and boil them, & put them into a frying pan with a dish of butter, & one or two onions, and so let them fry till they be brown all together, then cast a little salt upon them, and then serve them forth.'

TATTES OR BALDE MEATES FOR FISH DAIES
Thomas Dawson's *The Second part of The Good Huswifes Jewell*, 1597
'To make tattes or balde meates for fish daies. Take your dish and annoint the bottom well with butter, then make a fine pastry to the breadth of the dish. Lay it on the same dish upon the butter, then take beets, spinach and cabbages, or white lettuce, cutting them fine in long pieces. Then take the yolks of 8 raw eggs, and 6 yolks of hard eggs, with small raisins and a little cheese fine scraped, and grated bread, and 3 or 4 dishes of butter melted and clarified. When you have wrought it together, season it with sugar, cinnamon, ginger and salt. Then lay

it upon your fine pastry spreading it abroad, then the cover of fine pastry being cut with pretty work. Then set it in your oven. Bake it with your dish under it and when it is enough, then at the serving of it you must new paste the cover with butter, and so scrape sugar upon it, and then serve it forth.'

LAVER BREAD
Traditional

The seaweed called laver or purple laver is also known as black butter, purple sea-vegetable or sloke, and is *Porphyra umbilicalis*. In Chinese it is *jee choy*; in Gaelic it is *sleabchan, sleabhach* or *sleadai*; in Swedish it is *veckad purpurtang*. However, it is now best known, culinarily, as *nori*, the dried seaweed sheets used to wrap rolled sushi. It is harvested in winter at low tide, found attached to vertical surfaces such as rocks or piers. Laver is prepared in the UK by slow simmering, for as long as five hours, to form a thick gelatinous purée, and is available in cans or loose from South Wales markets. Known as Bara Lawr in Wales, it is usually served with bacon and/or cockles, the bacon being from the back rather than the side of the pig. It is also rolled with oatmeal into small laver cakes and fried in bacon fat, served with a traditional breakfast.

A FLORENTINE OF FISH – MOCK FISH FLORENTINE
A. W.'s *A Book of Cookrye*, 1584 and 1591

'A Florentine of Fish. Take apples, grated bread, currants, and chop your apples very fine, and mingle your stuff with yolks of eggs, and drive [roll] out your pastry as you do the other, put butter in your dish bottom and so serve it out.'

BOYLED SALLET

A. W.'s *A Book of Cookrye*, 1584 and 1591

'A boyled Sallet. Take spinach and boil it and chop it. When it is chopped, pour it in a little pipkin, with currants, sweet butter, vinegar and sugar. Boil them all together, and when they are boiled, put in a dish. Lay sippets round about, and strew sugar upon them and serve them out.'

COWCUMBER, LEMMON, EGGE AND HEARBE SALAD

Thomas Dawson's *The Good Huswifes Jewell*, 1596

'To make a Sallet of all kinde of hearbes. Take your herbs and pick them very fine into fair water. And pick your flowers by themselves, and wash them all clean, and swing them in a strainer. When you put them into a dish, mingle them with cucumbers or lemons paired and sliced, and scrape sugar, and put in vinegar and oil. Throw the flowers on the top of the salad, and of every sort of the aforesaid things, and garnish the dish about with the aforesaid things, and hard eggs boiled and laid about the dish and upon the salad.'

TO MAKE MEAT OF EGGES BEATEN

Epulario, or The Italian Banquet, 1598 translation of 1516 edition

'To make meat of Egges beaten, which shall shew like pease. Seethe eggs a little, then take them out of the broth and to make the broth somewhat thick, take the crumbs of a white loaf and strain it through the water. Or else take the broth of peas itself if you can get it, for it is better. And in any of these two broths you shall seethe your eggs again, with some spice, saffron, parsley and mint minced very small.'

TART OF SPINACH

Thomas Dawson's *The good Huswifes Handmaide for the Kitchin*, 1594

'To make a tart of Spinach. Take some cast cream, and seethe some spinach in fair water till it be very soft, then put it in a colander, that the water may soak from it. Then strain the spinach, and cast the cream together. Let there be good plenty of spinach. Set it upon a chafingdish of charcoal, and add to it sugar and some butter, and let it boil a while. Then put it in the paste, and bake it, and cast blanche powder on it, and so serve it.'

TARTE OF CHEESE

Thomas Dawson's *The good Huswifes Handmaide for the Kitchin*, 1594

'To make a tarte of Cheese. Make your tart, and then take Banbury Cheese. Pare away the outside of it. Cut the clean cheese in small pieces and put them into the tart, and when your tart is full of cheese, then put two handfuls of sugar into your tart upon your cheese. Cast in it five or six spoonfuls of rosewater, and close it up with a cover, and with a feather lay sweet molten butter upon it, and fine sugar, and bake it in a soft oven.'

[Banbury Cheese is still made, in very thin rounds, about an inch in thickness, with a sharp taste. It was a byword for anything unreasonably thin, with Bardolph calling Slender a 'Banbury cheese' in *The Merry Wives of Windsor*, written before 1597.]

FARSED EGGS – STUFFED EGGS

Thomas Dawson's *The Second part of The Good Huswifes Jewell*, 1597

'To farse Eggs. Take 8 or 10 eggs and boil them hard. Peel off the shells, and cut every egg in the middle then take out the yolks and make your stuffing as you do for meat, saving only you must put butter into it instead of suet. Fill your eggs where the yolks were, and then bind them and seethe them a little, and so serve them to the table.'

SMALL MEATS – SWEET VEGETARIAN PIES

Thomas Dawson's *The good Huswifes Handmaide for the Kitchin*, 1594

'To bake small meats. Take eggs and seethe them hard, then take the yolks out of them and bray [pound] them in a mortar, and temper them with cream. Then strain them, & put to them pepper, saffron, cloves, mace, small raisins, almonds blanched & small shred, & grated bread. Take pears also sodden in ale, & bray & strain them with the same liquor, and put thereto bastard* and honey. Put it in a pan and stir it on the fire till it be well sodden. Then make little coffins and set them in the oven until they be hard. Then you must take them out again, and put the aforesaid liquor into them, and so serve them forth.'

*A wine somewhere between sweet and astringent, also called 'mongrel'.

A SIMPLE PLAIN SALLET – MIXED SALAD WITH BOILED VEGETABLES

Gervase Markham's *The English Huswife*, 1615

'First then to speak of Sallets, there be some simple, some compounded, some only to furnish out the Table, and some both for use and adornation: your simple Sallets are Chibols pilled [peeled green onion], washt clean, and half of the green tops cut clean away, and so served on a fruit dish, or Chives, Scallions, Rhaddish roots, boyled Carrets, Skirrets and Turnips, with such like served up simply: Also, all young Lettuce, Cabbage-Lettuce, Purslane, and divers other herbs which may be served simply without any thing but a little Vinegar, Sallet Oyl and Sugar; Onions boyled; and stript from their rind, and served up with Vinegar, Oyl and Pepper, is a good simple Sallet; so is Camphire [samphire], Bean-cods [green beans], Sparagus, and Cucumbers, served in likewise with Oyl, Venegar and Pepper, with a world of others, too tedious to nominate.'

COVERED TART OF GREENE PEASE

Thomas Dawson's *The Good Huswifes Jewell*, 1596

'To make a close Tart of greene Pease. Take half a peck of green peas, shell them and seethe them, and cast them into a colander. Let the water go from them, then put them into the tart whole. Season them with pepper, saffron and salt, and a dish of sweet butter. Close and bake almost one hour, then draw out. Add a little verjuice, shake and set into the oven again, and so serve it.'

BLANCH MANGER FOR FISH DAYS

Thomas Dawson's *The Second part of The Good Huswifes Jewell*, 1597

'To make a blanch manger on the fish day. Take whites of eggs and cream, and boil them on a chafingdish on charcoal, till they curdle, then will their whey go from them. Then put away the whey, then put to the curd a little rosewater, then strain it and season it with sugar.'

STUED POTTAGE IN LENT
Thomas Dawson's *The good Huswifes Handmaide for the Kitchin*, 1594
'To make stued pottage in Lent. Take a fair pot, and fill it full of water, and take a saucer full of olive oil,* and put it into the pot. Then set your pot on the fire and let it boil. Then take parsley roots, and fennel roots, and scrape them clean, then cut them of the bigness of a Prune, and put them into the pot. Then take bread, and cut it in sops and cast it into a pot of wine: then strain it and put it in the pot. Then take rosemary, thyme and parsley, and bind them together, and put them into the pot. Then take dates, prunes, currants, and great raisins, and wash them clean, and put them in the pot. Then season your pot with salt, cloves, mace, and a little sugar. If it be not red enough, take saunders, and colour your pot therewith. Look that your broth be thick enough.'
*Older readers, like myself, will remember when olive oil was only available in pharmacies and the few delicatessens that existed in post-war Britain. Only since the 1980s has it been on sale in most supermarkets.

TARTE OF BEANES
A Proper New Booke of Cookery, 1545 and 1575
'To make a tart of Beanes. Take beans and boil them tender in fair water. Then take them out and break them in a mortar, and strain them with the yolks of 4 eggs, and curd made of milk. Then season it up with sugar and half a dish of butter, and a little cinnamon, and bake it.'

MACARONI AND COUSCOUS

Sir Hugh Plat's *Certaine Philosophical Preparations of Foode and Beverage for Sea-men*, 1607 (and Sundrie new and Artificiall remedies against Famine, 1595)

'And first for Food. A cheap, fresh and lasting victual, called by the name of Macaroni amongst the Italians, and not unlike (save only in form) to the Cus-cus [couscous] in Barbary [Morocco] may be upon reasonable warning provided in any quantity to serve either for change and variety of meat, or in the want of fresh victual. With this, the Author furnished Sir Francis Drake and Sir John Hawkins, in their last voyage.'

[This dish seems astonishing, but simply shows how adventurous Tudor cooking could be. Plat's cook's recipes date from Tudor times, and it is wonderful to think of Elizabethan privateers easting pasta. Plat extolled the virtues of macaroni and noted that the advantages of pasta as a food for seamen were that it kept well, even in hot conditions and it was relatively light in weight. On expeditions on land, one man could carry enough to feed two hundred men for a day. Pasta cooked quickly – a bonus to the cook in the tiny, cramped galley – and the saving in fuel translated to more saved space. It also was a welcome alternative to the salted meat staple of the seaman's diet. It served 'both in steede of bread and meate, wherby it performeth a double service'. Unused macaroni could be used to supply a second voyage, it lent itself to variation and enrichment and the ingredients for making it were available all year. Plat also knew of couscous, which has only become a regular item in UK supermarkets in the last fifteen years. Elizabeth Raffald in her 1769 *Experienced English House-Keeper* gave a recipe for 'Macaroni with Permasent (Parmesan) Cheese'.]

WHITE PEASE POTTAGE (WITH ADDED SEAL AND PORPOISE)

Thomas Dawson's *The Second part of The Good Huswifes Jewell*, 1597

'For White pease pottage. Take a quart of white peas* or more & seethe them in fair water close [covered], until they do cast their husks, the which cast away, as long as any will come up to the top. When they be gone, then put into the peas two dishes of butter, and a little verjuice, with pepper and salt, and a little fine powder of March**, and so let it stand till you will occupy it, and then serve it upon sops. You may see the porpoise and seal in your peas, serving it forth two pieces in a dish.'

*White peas are dried (or old) peas, similar to today's dried peas, which have to be soaked before use. They can be stored for a long time and therefore were useful on sea voyages.

**Powder of March (or Merchant's Powder) was a pre-ground seasoning made of a combination of several spices, such as pepper and ginger.

[If you have no ready access to a seal or porpoise, the above recipe can be made with 2 cups whole dried peas (or split peas) and 8–10 cups of water. Boil the peas in water until you achieve a thick pea soup consistency, adding more water if necessary. Taste peas and season to taste with butter, vinegar, pepper, salt and ginger, and serve over pieces of toasted bread.]

SPINAGE TART – SPINACH TART (1)

A Proper New Booke of Cookery, 1545 and 1575

'To make a Tart of Spinage. Take spinach and parboil it tender. Then take it up, and wring out the water clean, and chop it very small. Set it upon the fire with sweet butter in a frying pan. Season it, and set it in a platter to cool, than fill up your tart and so bake it.'

TARTE OF SPINADGE – SPINACH TART (2)

Thomas Dawson's *The Good Huswifes Jewell*, 1596

'To make a Tarte of Spinadge. Take spinach and seethe it stalk and all. When it is tenderly sodden, take it off, and let it drain in a colander and then swing it in a clowte [cloth].* Stamp it and strain it with two or three yolks of eggs, and then set it on a chafingdish of charcoal, and season it with butter and sugar. When the pastry is hardened in the oven, put in this commode, strake it even.'

*'Clout', or 'clowte', means cloth, from which we derive clothes, thereby the saying 'Cast not a clout till May is out' – i.e. keep your winter clothes on until the temperature warms.

SPINACH OR COLEWORTE TART (3)

Thomas Dawson's *The Second part of The Good Huswifes Jewell*, 1597

'To make a tarte of Spinach or of wheate leaves* or of colewortes. Take three handfuls of spinach, boil it in fair water, when it is boiled, put away the water from it and put the spinach in a stone mortar. Grind it small with two dishes of melted butter, and 4 raw eggs all to beat in. Then strain it and season it with sugar, cinnamon and ginger, and lay it in your coffin. When it is hardened in the oven, then bake it, and when it is enough cooked, serve it upon a fair dish, and cast upon it sugar and biscuits.

*This is a wasted resource for consumption, and the health benefits of coleworts such as kale and other *brassica* are only now being realised.

BUTTYRD WORTYS [GREENS] ON DICED BREAD

Gentyll Manly Cokere, MS Pepys 1047, *c.* 1490

'To make buttyrd Wortys. Take all maner of good herbs* that ye may get. Pick them, wash them and hack them and boil them up in fair water. And add thereto butter clarified a great quantity. And when they be boiled enough, salt them but let no oatmeal come therein. And dice bread in small gobbets & put it in dishes and pour the worts upon and serve it forth.'

*Herbs referred to any green edible plants.

FRITTORS OF SPINAGE

Thomas Dawson's *The good Huswifes Handmaide for the Kitchin*, 1594

'To make Frittors of Spinage. Take a good deale of spinach, and wash it clean, and boil it in fair water, and when it is boiled, put it in a colander, and let it cool. Then wring all the water out of it as near as ye can, lay it upon a board, and chop it with the back of a chopping knife very small. Put it in a platter, and add to it 4 whites of eggs, and 2 yolks, and the crumbs of half a manchet grated, and a little cinnamon & ginger. Stir them well together with a spoon. Take a frying pan and a dish of sweet butter in it, when it is molten put handsomely in your pan half a spoonful of your mixture, and so bestow the rest after. Fry them on a soft fire, and turn them when time is. Lay them in a platter and cast sugar on them.'

BAKED GLOBE ARTICHOKES

Thomas Dawson's *The Good Huswifes Jewell*, 1596

'To make a made dishe of Artechokes. Take your artichokes and pare away all the tops even to the meat. Boil them in sweet broth till they be some what tender. And then take them out, and put them into a dish, and seethe them with pepper, cinnamon and ginger. Then put in your dish that you mean to bake them in, and put in marrow to them a good store, and so let them bake. And when they be baked, put in a little vinegar and butter, and stick 3 or 4 leaves of the artichokes in the dish when you serve them up, and scrape sugar on the dish.'

CARRETS BOYLED

William Vaughan's *Approved Directions for Health, both Natural and Artificial: derived from the best physitians as well moderne as auncient*, 1612

'Carrets boyled and eaten with vinegar, Oyle, and Pepper serve for a special good salad to stirre up appetite, and to purifie blood.'

A SOP OF ONIONS OR SPINACH

Thomas Dawson's *The Second part of The Good Huswifes Jewell*, 1597

'A sop of Onions. Take and slice your onions, & put them in a frying pan with a dish or two of sweet butter, and fry them together. Then take a little fair water and put into it salt and pepper, and so fry them together a little more. Then boil them in a little earthenware pot, adding to it a little water and sweet butter, &c. You may use spinach in like manner.'

HOW TO MAKE A FRIED MEAT OF TURNEPS – BALDRICK'S SURPRISE

Epulario, or The Italian Banquet, 1598 translation of 1516 edition

'How to make a fried meat of turneps. Roast the turnips in the embers or else boil them whole, then cut or slice them in pieces as thick as half the shaft of a knife. Which done, take cheese and cut it in the same form and quantity, but somewhat thinner. Then take sugar, pepper, and other spices mingled together, and put them in a pan under the pieces of cheese, as if you would make a crust under the cheese, and on top of them likewise. And over it you shall lay the pieces of turnips, covering them over with the spices aforesaid, and plenty of good butter. And so you shall do with the said cheese and turnips till the pan be full, letting them cook the space of a quarter of an hour, or more, like a tart, and this would be one of your last dishes. [The last sentence refers to the fact that the cook can prepare this hot at the last moment for a banquet.]

OATMEAL CAWDLE
Thomas Dawson's *The Second part of The Good Huswifes Jewell*, 1597
'To make a cawdle of Ote meale. Take two handfuls or more of great oatmeal, and beat it in a stone mortar well. Then put it into a quart of ale, and set it on the fire, and stir it. Season it with cloves, mace, and sugar beaten, and let it boil till it be enough, and then serve it forth upon sops.'
[Bread features in many, many dishes, being the main and necessary carbohydrate for all classes before the advent of potatoes from the New World.]

BOILED SPICED ONIONS ON BREAD
Thomas Dawson's *The Second part of The Good Huswifes Jewell*, 1597
'To boil Onions. Take a good many onions and cut them in four quarters, and set them on the fire in as much water as you think will boil them tender. And when they be

clean skimmed, put in a good many of small raisins, half a spoonful of grosse pepper, a good piece of sugar, and a little salt. And when the onions be thoroughly boiled, beat the yolk of an egg with verjuice, and add into your pot and so serve it upon sops. If you wish, poach eggs and lay upon them.'

6

Savoury Delights

MISTRESSE DRAKE'S WAY TO MAKE SOFT CHEESE ALL THE YEAR

Thomas Dawson's *The good Huswifes Handmaide for the Kitchin*, 1594

'Mistresse Drakes way to make soft Cheese all the yeare through, that it shall be lyke rowen Cheese.* Take your milk as it cometh from the cow, and put it in a vessel till it be cold, then take as much fair water, and set it on the fire. When your water is warm, add so much of your water in that milk as will warm the milk. Then take a spoonful of runt [rennet] and more, and put into your milk and make your cheese, and put it into a fair cloth. And so put it into the press, & turn it in the press often, and wipe it with fair cloths as often as ye turn it.'

*Rowan cheese was much prized, being produced from animals that had fed on grass that sprang up in the autumn meadows after summer mowing. The milk from this fodder produced a curd which retained moisture and had a particular flavour and texture. In his *Dietary of Health* (1542), Andrew Boorde gave us seven types of cheese known in medieval England. As well as rowan cheese, there was 'green cheese', green in the sense of being new. It was made from either whole or semi-skimmed milk and was eaten in a fairly fresh state. It was pressed sufficiently to retain its shape but was still moist and probably similar to today's Lancashire and Caerphilly cheeses, which ripen with a few weeks. 'Soft cheese' was again made from either whole or semi-skimmed milk and turned out similarly to today's regional cheeses such as Cheddar, Cheshire and Double Gloucester. They were firm and waxy in texture and were called soft because they were in comparison to 'hard cheese'. This was the staple cheese of the poor, made from skimmed milk, and its low-fat content meant that it kept well. However, it was quite tough and its texture may have resembled Parmesan cheese. The fifth cheese variety was 'spermyse', made with additions such as herbs and herb juices, such as Sage Derby cheese, but we know little of other varieties. Curd cheese was made overnight, using sour milk. There will also have been blue cheeses, of which perhaps 'Blue Vinny' is a survivor.

TART OF CHEESE (1)
A Proper New Booke of Cookery, 1545 and 1575
'To make a Tart of Cheese. Take hard cheese and cut it in slices, and pare it, then lay it in faire water, or in sweet milk, for the space of 3 hours. Then take it up, and break it in a mortar till it be small, then draw it up through a strainer, with the yolks of 6 eggs, and season it with sugar and sweet butter, and so bake it.'

TARTE OF CHEESE (2)
A. W.'s *A Book of Cookrye*, 1584 and 1591
'To make a Tarte of Cheese. Take good fine pastry and drive [roll] it as thin as you can. Then take cheese, pare it, mince it, and bray it in a mortar with the yolks of eggs

till it be like pastry. Then put it in a fair dish with clarified butter, and then put it abroad into your pastry and cover it with a fair cut cover, and so bake it. That done, serve it forth.'

CURDE FRITTORS – CURD CRÈPES
Thomas Dawson's *The good Huswifes Handmaide for the Kitchin*, 1594

'To make Curde Frittors. Take the yolks of 10 eggs, and break them in a pan. Add to them one handful of curds and one handful of fine flour, and strain them all together, and make a batter. And if it be not thick enough, put more curds in it, and add salt to it. Then set it on the fire in a frying pan, with such stuff as ye will fry them with, and when it is hot, with a ladle take part of your batter, and put it into the pan, and let it run as small as you can [try for the thinnest layer possible spread across the pan]. Stir then with a stick, and turn them with a scummer [skimmer], and when they be fair and yellow fried, take them out, and cast sugar upon them, and serve them forth.'

[These fritters are similar to thin pancakes or crèpes. Use 5 eggs; curds (soft cheese such as ricotta or cottage cheese); wheat flour; salt; sugar. Make a thin batter with the eggs and equal amounts of curds and flour, seasoning with salt. Heat a small amount of butter in your frying pan. When hot, pour in the batter and tip the pan to make the batter spread very thinly. When brown on one side, use a spatula to flip them over, or slide them on to a plate and flip them over into the pan. Add more butter (or oil) to the pan when needed. Serve with sugar sprinkled on the top if you wish.]

FRESH GINGER AND ROSEWATER CHEESE AND CLOTTED CREAM

Thomas Dawson's *The Good Huswifes Jewell*, 1596

'To make a fresh Cheese and Creame. Take a gallon or two of milk from the cow and seethe it, and when it doth seethe, put thereunto a quart or two of morning milk in fair cleansing pans, in such a place as no dust may fall therein. And this is for your clowted [clotted] cream. The next morning take a quart of morning milk, and seethe it, and when it doth seethe, put in a quart of cream thereunto, and take it off the fire. Put it into a faire earthenware pan. Let it stand until it be somewhat blood warm, but first over night put a good quantity of ginger, with rosewater, and stir it together, and let it settle all night. The next day put it into your said blood-warm milk to make your cheese come, then put the curds in a fair cloth, with a little good rosewater, and stir in powder of ginger, and a little sugar. So last, tie great soft towels together with a thread and crush out the whey with your clotted cream, and mix it with fine powder of ginger, and sugar, and so sprinkle it with rosewater, and put your cheese in a fair dish, and put these cloths round about it. Then take a pint of raw milk or cream, and put it in a pot, and all to shake it, until it be gathered into a froth like snow. And ever as it comes, take it off with a spoon, and put it into a colander. Then put it upon your fresh cheese, and prick it with wafers, and so serve it.'

FRESH CHEESE

The Good Hous-wiues Treasurie, 1588

'To make fresh Cheese. Take new milk and put a litle running [rennet] to it, and when it is skimmed break it. Then take some sugar, cinnamon & rosewater, and so put it in a cheese mould, and put cream to it.'

EGS UPON SOPS

Thomas Dawson's *The good Huswifes Handmaide for the Kitchin*, 1594

'To make Egs upon Sops. Take eggs and poach them as soft as ye can. Then take a fine manchet, and make sops thereof, and put your sops in a dish. And put verjuice thereto and sugar and a little butter. Then set it to the fire, and let it boil. Then take your eggs and lay them upon your sops, and cast a little chopped parsley upon them, and so serve them.'

FYSTES OF PORTINGALE – PORTUGUESE TENNIS BALLS

Thomas Dawson's *The good Huswifes Handmaide for the Kitchin*, 1594

'How to make Fystes of Portingale'. Take some sweet suet minced small, the yolks of two eggs, with grated bread and currants. Temper all these together with a little saffron, cinnamon, ginger, and a little salt. Then seethe them in a little Bastard or Sack [fortified wine like sherry] a little while. And when they have boiled a little take it up, and cast some sugar to it, & so make balls of it as big as tennis balls, & lay 4 or 5 in a dish, and pour on some of the broth that they were sodden in, and so serve them.'

FINE PAPPE POTTAGE

Thomas Dawson's *The good Huswifes Handmaide for the Kitchin*, 1594

'How to make fine pappe. Take milk and flour. Strain them, and set over the fire till it boils. Then take it off and let it cool, then take the yolks of eggs, strain them and put in the milk, and some salt, and set it in the fire. Stir it till it be thick, and let it not boil fully. Then put it in a dish abroad, and serve it forth for good pottage.'

A TANSIE – WALNUT LEAF OMELETTE
The Good Hous-wiues Treasurie, 1588

'For a Tansie. Take either walnut tree leaves* or lettuce alone, or all other good herbs, stamp them and strain them and take a little cream and grated bread, nutmeg, pepper and sugar, 4 eggs, 2 of the whites. Beat them together and so fry it in a pan.'

*As with wheat leaves above, the Tudors used anything edible – their cuisine was more adventurous than we realise.

DEVISED MEAT AFTER THE ROMANE MANNER – RIGATONI WITH CHEESE SAUCE
Epulario, or The Italian Banquet, 1598 translation of 1516 edition

'Take white flour, and make paste of it somewhat thicker than a pancake, and roll it about a staff. Then take out the staff, then cut the pastry in pieces of the length of thy little finger, whereby they will be hollow like a pudding and round or close. Then seethe them in fat broth or in water as time serveth, but the broth or water must be boiling when you put them in. And if you seethe them in water put a little sweet [unsalted] butter and salt it, and when they are cooked, dish them with cheese, butter, and spices.'

[This author never knew pasta until the 1960s, and still knows people who have never tasted pasta – nor Indian nor Chinese food ...]

GALLENTINE

Thomas Dawson's *The good Huswifes Handmaide for the Kitchin*, 1594

'To make Gallentine. Take toasts of white bread, boil them on a chafingdish of charcoal, with vinegar, when it hath soaked afore in the vinegar. In the boiling put in a branch of rosemary, sugar, cinnamon and ginger, strain it and serve it.'

FRIED SPINACH TOASTIES

Thomas Dawson's *The Second part of The Good Huswifes Jewell*, 1597

'To make fried toast of Spinage. Take spinach and seethe it in water and salt, and when it is tender, wring out the water between two [wooden] trenchers. Then chop it small and set it on a chafingdish of charcoal. Add thereto butter, small raisins, cinnamon, ginger and sugar, and a little of the juice of an orange and 2 yolks of raw eggs. Let it boil till it be somewhat thick, then toast your toast, soak them in a little butter, and sugar, and spread thinly your spinach upon them, and set them on a dish before the fire a little while. And so serve them with a little sugar upon them.

EGGES YN BREWTE – EGGS POACHED IN MILK, WITH CHEESE TOPPING

Gentyll Manly Cokere, MS Pepys 1047, *c.* 1490

'Egges yn brewte. Take water and seethe it. In the same water break your eggs and cast therein ginger, pepper and saffron, then temper it up with sweet milk and boil it. And then carve cheese and cast thereto small cut. And when it is enough serve it forth.'

MORTIS – TUDOR CHICKEN PATÉ

Thomas Dawson's *The Good Huswifes Jewell*, 1596

'To make a mortis. Take almonds and blanch them, and beat them in a mortar. Boil a chicken, and take all the flesh off him, and beat it, and strain them together, with milk and water, and so put them into a pot. Put in sugar, and still stir them, and when it hath boiled a good while, take it off. Set it a cooling in a pail of water, and strain it again with rosewater into a dish.'

FRESH CHEESE WITH CINNAMON AND GINGER

A Closet for Ladies and Gentlewomen, 1602

'To make a fresh Cheese. Take a quantity of new milk, and set it on the fire. Let it boil, and take half a dozen yolks of eggs, and beat them and stir them in the milk on the fire. Then take it off the fire, and keep it stirred, until it be lukewarm. Then put runnet [rennet] into it, and stir it, and let it stand until it be gathered together & take up the curd. And put into it cinnamon and ginger, and stir it about, & make dishes of it, as you think good.'

TARTS OWTE OF LENTE – EGG AND CHEESE TART

Gentyll Manly Cokere, MS Pepys 1047, *c.* 1490

'For tarts owte of lente. Take neshe [soft] cheese and pare it and grind it in a mortar. Break eggs and add thereto and then put in butter and cream and mix all well together. Put not too much butter therein if the cheese be fat. Make a coffin of dough and close it above with dough and colour it above with the yolks of eggs. Bake it well and serve it forth.'

SAUSEDGE

Thomas Dawson's *The Good Huswifes Jewell*, 1596

'To make a sausedge. Take Martinmass beef*, or if you cannot get it, take fresh beef, or the lean of bacon if you will, & you must mince very small that kind of flesh that you take. Cut lard & put into the minced meat, and whole pepper, and the yolks of 7 eggs, and mingle them altogether. Put the meat into a gut very salted, and hang it in the chimney where it may dry, and there let him hang a month or two before you take him down.'

*'Martinmasse beefe' was dried, salted beef, it being common practice to slaughter cattle on the feast-day of St Martin, 11 November, to be preserved for winter. Historically, hiring fairs were held on this day, when farm labourers would seek new posts.

SPINACH BALL FRITTERS

Thomas Dawson's *The Good Huswifes Jewell*, 1596

'To make Fritters of Spinnedge. Take a good deal of spinach, and wash it clean, then boil it in fair water. When it is boiled, then take it forth and let the water run from it. Then chop it with the back of a knife, and then put in some eggs and grated bread, and season it with sugar, cinnamon, ginger and pepper, dates minced finely, and currants, and roll them like a ball, and dip them in batter made of ale and flour.'

UNIVERSAL STUFFING

Thomas Dawson's *The Second part of The Good Huswifes Jewell*, 1597

'To farse all things. Take a good handful of thyme, hyssop, parsley, and 3 or 4 yolks of eggs hard roasted, and chop them with herbs small. Then take white bread grated and raw eggs with sweet butter, a few small raisins, or barberries, seasoning it with pepper, cloves, mace, cinnamon and ginger, working it altogether as paste, and then may you stuff with it what you will.'

FRITTER STUFFE
Thomas Dawson's *The Good Huswifes Jewell*, 1596
'To make Fritter stuffe. Take fine flour, and 3 or 4 eggs, and put into the flour, and a piece of butter, and let them boil all together in a dish or chafer. Add in sugar, cinnamon, ginger and rosewater. In the boiling, add in a little grated bread to make it big, and then put it into a dish. Beat it well together, and so put it into your mould, and fry it with clarified butter, but your butter may not be too hot nor too cold.'

FRITTERS
The Good Hous-wiues Treasurie, 1588
'To make Fritters. Take a little fair warm water, as much sack [wine], and take half flour and half bread. Mingle them all together. Then take 5 or 6 eggs and break therein whites and all, a little nutmeg, pepper and salt, and cut in apples very small. Then take a fair skillet with suet and let it boil on the fire and so put the batter in it.'

PURSES OR CREMITARIES
Thomas Dawson's *The Second part of The Good Huswifes Jewell*, 1597
'To make purses or cremitaries. Take a little marrow, small raisins & dates. Let the stones be taken away, these being beaten together in a mortar. Season with ginger, cinnamon

and sugar, then put it in small fine pastry cases. Bake them or fry them, so done in the serving of them cast blaunch pouder upon them.'

FRIANS
Thomas Dawson's *The good Huswifes Handmaide for the Kitchin*, 1594
'To make Frians. Take 3 handfuls of flour, 7 yolks of eggs, and half a dish of butter. Make your pastry therewith and make 2 chewets thereof, as you would make 2 Tarts. And when it is driven very fine with your rolling pin, then cut them in pieces of the bigness of your hand. Then take a quartern of sugar, and one ounce and four spoonfuls of cinnamon, and half a spoonful of ginger, and mingle them altogether. Then take lumps of marrow, of the quantity of your finger, and put it on your pieces of pastry afore rehearsed. Put upon it 2 spoonfuls of your sugar and spices. Then take a little water and wet your paste therewith. Then make them even as you would make a pasty of venison. Then prick them with a pin, and fry them as ye fry fritters. When they be fried, cast a little sugar on them, and so serve them.'

EGGS IN MONE SHINE – MOONSHINE EGGS
A Proper New Booke of Cookery, 1545 and 1575
'To make egges in mone shine. Take a dish of rosewater, and a dish full of sugar, and set them upon a chafingdish, and let them boil. Then take the yolks of 8 or 9 eggs newly laid, and add them thereto, every one from other, and so let them harden a little. And so after this manner serve them forth, and cast a little cinnamon and sugar.'

16. A sixteenth-century illustration by Hoefnagel, showing some peaches.

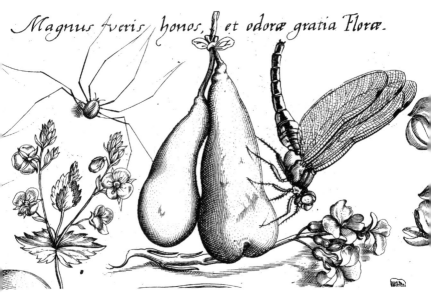

Magnus veris honos, et odoræ gratia Floræ.

17. A sixteenth-century illustration of a pear by Hoefnagel. Hundreds of varieties of pear have now been lost.

7

Fruit Dishes

PEAR PIES
A. W.'s *A Book of Cookrye*, 1584 and 1591
'How to bake Wardens [sour green pears]. Core your wardens and pare them, and parboil them and lay them in your pastry, and put in every warden where you take out the core a clove or two. Add to them sugar, ginger, cinnamon, more cinnamon than ginger. Make your crust very fine and somewhat thick, and bake them leisurely.'

PEAR TART
Thomas Dawson's *The Good Huswifes Jewell*, 1596
'To make a Tarte of Wardens. You must bake your wardens first in a pie, and then take all the wardens and cut them in 4 quarters, and core them. Put them into a tart pinched, with your sugar, and season them with sugar, cinnamon and ginger, and set them in the oven. Put no cover on them, but you must cut a cover and lay in the tart when it is baked. Butter the tart and the cover too, and adorn it with sugar.'

BAKED PEARES, QUINCES AND WARDENS

Thomas Dawson's *The good Huswifes Handmaide for the Kitchin*, 1594

'To bake Peares, quinces, and wardens. You must take and pare them, and then core them. Then make your pastry with fair water and butter, and the yolk of an egg, and set your oranges into the pastry, and then bake it well. Then fill your pastry almost full with cinnamon, ginger and sugar. Also apples must be taken after the same way, saving that whereas the core should be cut out, they must be filled with butter every one. The hardest apples are best, and likewise are pears and wardens, and none of them all but the wardens may be parboiled, and the oven must be of a temperate heat, 2 hours to stand is enough.'

[Dawson exactly repeats this recipe in his *The Good Huswifes Jewell*, 1596.]

PEACH PIES

Thomas Dawson's *The good Huswifes Handmaide for the Kitchin*, 1594

'To bake Peaches. Take peaches, pare them, and cut them in two pieces. Take out the stones as clean as you can for breaching of the peach. Then make your pie 3 square to bake 4 in a pie. Let your pastry be very fine, then make your dredge with fine sugar, cinnamon and ginger. First lay a little dredge in the bottom of your pies. Then put in peaches, and fill up your coffins with your dredge, and put into every coffin 3 spoonfuls of rosewater. Let not your oven be too hot.'

TO PRESERVE ORENGES IN SIRROPPE

Thomas Dawson's *The Good Huswifes Jewell*, 1596

'To preserve Orenges. You must cut your oranges in half and pare them a little round about, and let them lie in water 4 or 5 days. You must change the water once or twice a day, and when you preserve them, you must have a quarter of faire water to put in your sugar, and a little rosewater, and set it on the fire. Skim it very clean, and put in a little cinnamon, and put in your orange. Let them boil a little while, and then take them out again, and do so 5 or 6 times, and when they be enough, put in your oranges and let your syrup stand till it be cold, and then put your syrup into your oranges.'

TARTE OF APPLES AND ORANGE PEELS

Thomas Dawson's *The good Huswifes Handmaide for the Kitchin*, 1594

'To make a tarte of apples and Orange peels. Take your oranges, and lay them in water a day and a night, then seethe them in fair water and honey. Let them seethe till they be soft. Then let them soak in the syrup a day and a night. Then take them forth and cut them small, and then make your tart and season your apples with sugar, cinnamon and ginger, and put in a piece of butter. Lay a course of apples, and between the same course of apples, a course of oranges, and so course by course. And season your oranges as you seasoned your apples, with somewhat more sugar,* then lay on the lid and put it in the oven. When it is almost baked, take rosewater and sugar, and boil them together till it be somewhat thick, then take out the tart. Take a feather and spread the rosewater and sugar on the lid, and set it into the oven again, and let the sugar harden on the lid, and let it not burn.

* At this time oranges were small Seville oranges, and very bitter.

PIPPEN PYE

The Good Hous-wiues Treasurie, 1588

'To make a Pippen Pye. Take a dozen of faire pippins [apples], a pound of sugar in the crust and pie, half an ounce of cinnamon, 2 orange peels shred fine, 2 spoonfuls of rosewater. Then heat your oven and let it stand in 2 hours or 2 and a half, and make a vent in the lid thereof. This pie is good when the quince is out of season.'

APPLE PIES

Thomas Dawson's *The good Huswifes Handmaide for the Kitchin*, 1594

'To bake pippins. Take your pippins and pare them, and make your coffin of fine pastry, and cast a little sugar in the bottom of the pie. Then put in your pippins, and set them as close as ye can. Then take sugar, cinnamon and ginger, and make them in a dredge, and fill the pie therewith. Close it, and let it bake 2 hours but the oven must not be too hot.'

APPLE TART

Thomas Dawson's *The Second part of The Good Huswifes Jewell*, 1597

'A tarte of appels. Make your coffin 2 inches deep round about, then take 10 or 12 good apples. Pare them and slice them, and put them into the pastry with 2 dishes of butter among the apples. Cover your tart close with the pastry, and break a dish of butter in pieces, and lay it upon the cover because of burning in the pan. And when the apples be tender, take it forth and cut off the cover, & beat the apples together till they be soft, and if they be dry put the more butter into them. And so season them with cinnamon, ginger and sugar, then must you cut your cover after the fashion, leaving it upon your tarts. Serve it with blaunch powder.'

GREEN APPLE PIES

A Proper New Booke of Cookery, 1545 and 1575

'To make pies of greene Apples. Take your apples and pare them clean, and core them as ye will a quince. Then make your coffin after this manner, take a little fair water, and half a dish of butter, and a little saffron, and set all this upon a chafingdish, till it be hot. Then temper your flour with this said liquor, and the white of 2 eggs, & also make your coffin and season your apples with cinnamon, ginger and sugar enough. Then put them into your coffin, and bake them.'

18. An apple, rosebud, skirret and berries, as seen in a sixteenth-century engraving by Hoefnagel.

Qnod inuocatus lubenter cœnito! Musca sum.

CITRON PIE (1)

Thomas Dawson's *The Second part of The Good Huswifes Jewell*, 1597

'To bake a Citron pie. Take your citron*, pare it and slice it in pieces, and boil it with grose pepper and ginger, and so lay it in your pastry with butter. When it is almost baked put thereto vinegar, butter and sugar, and let it stand in the oven a while and soak.'

*A lemon is usually yellow or light green, and its usual purpose in cooking is in its flavouring and acid juice. It has a leathery type of skin, is quite aromatic, and has a juicy pulp. The distinctive sour taste makes lemons a favourite ingredient in cooking and baking. All parts of this fruit are used, that is, the lemon juice, the rind, and the zest are used, and its juice is excellent for marinating pork and fish. The juice is also used as a short-term preservative on certain foods like apples, bananas, and avocados, because once sliced, lemons turn brown. A citron, while similarly a fragrant citrus fruit, consists of a dry pulp and only a small quantity of insipid juice. Citrons have a variety of shapes, and the citron was used mainly for medicinal purposes. It was greatly used to fight seasickness, intestinal problems, pulmonary illnesses and many other things. The oil that is taken from the pulp, or the outermost layer of the rind, is actually used as an antibiotic. So unlike lemons, the citron is prized for its outermost yellow rind. However, the Tudors used them in cooking. It is now difficult to find citrons in England, but southern Italy is known for citron candies and many citron products.

CITRON PIE (2)
Thomas Dawson's *The Second part of The Good Huswifes Jewell*, 1597
'Another way to bake Citrons. When your citrons be pared & sliced, lay it in your pastry with small raisins, and season them with pepper, ginger, and fine sugar.'

BOILED SPICED CITRONS
Thomas Dawson's *The Second part of The Good Huswifes Jewell*, 1597
'To boil Citrons. When your citrons be boiled, pared and sliced, seethe them with water and wine, and put to them butter, small raisins, barberries, sugar, cinnamon and ginger, and let them seethe till your citrons be tender.'

SALLET OF LEMMONS
Thomas Dawson's *The Good Huswifes Jewell*, 1596
'To make a Sallet of Lemmons. Cut out slices of the peel of the lemons longways, a quarter of an inch one piece from another. Then slice the lemon very thin. Lay the lemons in a dish in a cross, and the peels about the lemons, and scrape a good deal of sugar upon them, and so serve them.'

ANY FRUIT TART
Thomas Dawson's *The Good Huswifes Jewell*, 1596
'To make all maner of fruit Tarte. You must boil your fruit, whether it be apple, cherry, peach, damson, pear, mulberry, or codling [apple], in fair water. When they be boiled enough, put them into a bowl, and bruise them with a ladle, and when they be cold, strain them. Add

in red wine or Claret wine, and so season it with sugar, cinnamon and ginger.'

A TARTE OF GOSEBERRIES
A Proper New Booke of Cookery, 1545 and 1575
'To make a tarte of Goseberies. Take gooseberries and parboil them in white wine, claret or ale, and boil withall a little white bread. Then take them up and draw them through a strainer as thick as you can, with the yolks of 5 eggs. Then season it up with sugar and half a dish of butter, to bake it.'

TARTE OF MEDLARS
A Proper New Booke of Cookery, 1545 and 1575
'To bake a Tarte of Medlars. Take medlars when they be rotten*, & bray them with the yolks of 4 eggs, then season it up with sugar and cinnamon and sweet butter, and so bake it.'
*Medlars must be decaying to release their sweetness – the term is 'bletted'.

A TARTE OF PRUNES (1)
A. W.'s *A Book of Cookrye*, 1584 and 1591
'To make a Tarte of Prunes. Take prunes and wash them, then boil them with fair water. Cut in half a penny loaf of white bread, and take them out and strain them with Claret wine. Season it with cinnamon, ginger and sugar, and a little rosewater. Make the pastry as fine as you can, and dry it, and fill it, and let it dry in the oven. Take it out and cast on it biscuits* and caraways.'
*Biscuits would be slices of 'bisket bread' – see later recipe.

TARTE OF PRUNES (2)

Thomas Dawson's *The Good Huswifes Jewell*, 1596

'To make a Tarte of Prunes. Put your Prunes into a pot, and put in red wine or claret wine, and a little faire water, and stir them now and then, and when they be boiled enough, put them into a bowl, and strain them with sugar, cinnamon and ginger.'

DAMSON AND PEAR TART

A Proper New Booke of Cookery, 1545 and 1575

'To make a Tart of Damsons. Take damsons* and boil them in wine, either red or claret, and put thereto a dozen of pears, or else white bread to make them stuff withall, then draw them up with the yolks of 6 eggs, and sweet butter, and so bake it.'

*One sees damson trees especially round old farmsteads. The damson is a subspecies of the plum, and differs in form. Plums are rounded and they have a more pronounced fruit-cheek. Their colour varies from blue, red and purple to black. Their flesh tastes sweet and juicy and has a fluffy consistency and is difficult to remove from the kernel. Damsons (*Prunus domestica*) are oblong/oval and smaller than plums, and always have a skin which ranges from dark blue to indigo to nearly black. Moreover they have a firmer and drier flesh. They have a sweet-sour taste and the flesh is easy to remove from the kernel. They also differ fundamentally in the processing. Plums are very often used to make marmalade or compote or they are eaten freshly. The damson fruit flesh does not disintegrate during cooking or baking because of its low water content, so is often used for cakes or cooking recipes. Damson jam is excellent, and damson gin needs far less sugar than sloe gin.

TART OF CHERIES (1)
A Proper New Booke of Cookery, 1545 and 1575

'To make a Tart of Cheries. Take all things that ye do to the tart of damsons, but ye add no pears.'

TART OF CHERIES (2)
Thomas Dawson's *The good Huswifes Handmaide for the Kitchin*, 1594

'To make a good tart of Cheries. Take your cherries and pick out the stones of them. Then take raw yolks of eggs, and put them into your cherries. Then take sugar, cinnamon and ginger, and cloves, and add to your cherries & make your tart with all the eggs. Your tart must be of an inch high, when it is made put in your cherries without any liquor, and cast sugar, cinnamon and ginger upon it, and close it up. Lay it on a paper, & put it in the oven. When it is half baked draw it out, and put the liquor that you let off your cherries into the tart. Then take molten butter, and with a feather anoint your lid therewith. Then take fine beaten sugar and cast upon it. Then put your tarte into the oven again, and let it bake a good while. When it is baked draw it forth, & cast sugar & rosewater upon it, and serve it.'

TART OF CHERIES (3)
Thomas Dawson's *The good Huswifes Handmaide for the Kitchin*, 1594

'To make a Tart of Cherries, when the stones be out, another waye. Seethe them in white wine or in Claret, and drain them thick: when they be sodden: then take two yolks of eggs & thicken it withall. Then season it with cinnamon, ginger and sugar, and bake it, and so serve it.'

TARTES OF RED CHERRIES – ROSE AND CHERRY CHEESECAKE

Epulario, or The Italian Banquet, 1598 translation of 1516 edition

'To make Tartes of red Cherries. Take the reddest cherries that may be got. Take out the stones and stamp them in a mortar. Then take red roses chopped with a knife, with a little new cheese and some old cheese well stamped with cinnamon, ginger, pepper and sugar, and all this mixed together. Add thereunto some eggs according to the quantity you will make, and with a crust of pastry bake it in a pan. Being baked, strew it with sugar and rosewater.'

BORAGE FLOWER or APPLE TART

A Proper New Booke of Cookery, 1545 and 1575

'To make a Tart of Bourage Flowers. Take borage flowers* and parboil them tender, then strain them with the yolks of 3 or 4 eggs and sweet curds. Or else take 3 or 4 apples,

19. An Elizabethan fruit trencher, a small wooden tray for fruit. The decoration was for show - diners ate off the other side, which was plain and could be scrubbed.

and parboil withall, and strain them with sweet butter, and a little mace, and so bake it.'

*Borage is easy to grow and self-seeds – the pale-blue, star-like small flowers can be put in ice cubes for drinks like Pimms.

MARYGOLDES, PRIM ROSES AND COUSLIPS TART
A Proper New Booke of Cookery, 1545 and 1575

'To make a Tart of Marygoldes, prim roses, or Couslips. Take the same stuff to every of them that you do to the tart of borage [above] and the same seasoning.'

STRAWBERRY TART
A Proper New Booke of Cookery, 1545 and 1575

'To make a Tart of Strawberies. Take and strain them with the yolks of 4 eggs, and a little white bread grated, then season it up with sugar, and sweet butter, and so bake it.'

8

Desserts and Sweets

Sugar was a fantastically expensive luxury during the Middle Ages, arriving at ports crystallised in rock-hard cones. These had to be hacked into smaller pieces, before being laboriously ground to a powder in a pestle and mortar. During the sixteenth century more and more elaborate means of working sugar were discovered, and it became the basis for both wet and dry 'suckets', variants on crystallised fruit and fruit pulps. It was discovered that adding gum tragacanth in a rosewater solution to the sugar created a mouldable sugar paste and this could be used to make more and more fanciful subtleties or edible models, such as one of St Paul's which was presented to Elizabeth I.

BANQUETING NECESSITIES
Thomas Dawson's *The good Huswifes Handmaide for the Kitchin*, 1594
'All necessaries appertaining to a Banquet. Cinnamon, Sugar, Nutmegs, Pepper, Saffron, Saunders, Coleander, Anniseeds, Licoras, all kind of Comfets, Oranges, Pomegranate, Tornsall [turnsole], Lemmans, Prunes, Currants, Barberries conserved, Paper white and browne: seeds, Rosewater, Raisins, Rie flower [Rye flour], Ginger,

Cloves and mace, Damaske water [rose water from *rosa Damascena*], Dates, Cherries conserved, sweet Oranges, Wafers for your Marchpanes, seasoned and unseasoned, Spinnedges.'

COVER TARTE AFTER THE FRENCHE FASHION
A Proper New Booke of Cookery, 1545 and 1575
'To make a cover Tarte after the Frenche fashion. Take a pint of cream and the yolks of 10 eggs, and beat them all together. Add thereto half a dish of sweet butter, and sugar, and boil them till they be thick. Then take them up and cool them in a platter, and make a couple of cakes of fine pastry, and lay your stuff in one of them. Cover it with the other, and cut the vent above, and so bake it.'

SWEET POTATOES IN ROSE AND ORANGE SYRUP
Elinor Fettiplace's *Receipt Book*, 1604
'Boil your roots in fair water until they be somewhat tender, then peel off the skin. Then make your syrup, weighing to every pound of roots a pound of sugar and a quarter of a pint of fair water, & as much of rosewater, & the juice of 3 or 4 oranges. Then boil the syrup, & boil them till they be thoroughly soaked in the syrup, before you take it from the fire, put in a little musk and amber Greece [ambergris].'
[Sweet potatoes have only in the last ten years become a normal item in supermarkets, and are a healthier alternative to potatoes in savoury dishes, but here we see a dessert dish. Ambergris is a waxy substance found floating at sea, or washed up on beaches, secreted by the sperm whale and still of great value in perfume manufacture. It was

often spelt amber grease/greece, signifying its colour and function, and was sometimes mixed with salt in cooking.]

A TART OF EGGS
Thomas Dawson's *The Second part of The Good Huswifes Jewell*, 1597
'A tart of eggs. Take 12 eggs and butter them together, then strain them with rosewater. Season it with Sugar, then put it into your pastry, and so bake it and serve it with sugar upon it.'

A POSSET
The Good Hous-wiues Treasurie, 1588
'For a Posset. Take a posnet [a porringer, or small basin] full of cream and seethe it and put sugar and cinnamon in it. Then take half ale and half Sack [sweet fortified wine] and add sugar and cinnamon in it.'

CLOWTED CREAM AFTER MISTRES HORSMANS WAY
Thomas Dawson's *The good Huswifes Handmaide for the Kitchin*, 1594
'To make clowted Cream after Mistres Horsmans way. When you have taken the milk from the cow, straight set it on the fire, but see that your fire be without smoke, and a soft fire. And so keep it on from morning till it be night, or nigh thereabout, and ye must be sure that it doth not seethe all that while, and ye must let your milk be set on the fire, in as broad a vessel as you can. Then take it from the fire, and set it upon a board, and let it stand al night. Then in the morning take off the cream, and put it in a dish or where ye will.'

APPELMOISE (1)

A Proper New Booke of Cookery, 1545 and 1575

'To make an Appelmoise. Take a dozen apples, and roast or boil them, and draw them through a strainer, and the yolks of 3 or 4 eggs withall. As ye strain them, temper them with 3 or 4 spoonfuls of damask water [rosewater made from damask roses], if ye will, then take and season it with sugar and half a dish of sweet butter. Boil them upon a chafingdish in a platter. Cast biskets [biscuits] or cinnamon and ginger upon them, and so serve them forth.'

APPILLINOSE – APPLEMUSE (2)

A Noble Boke off Cookry ffor a Prynce Houssolde Holkham, MSS 674, 1480/1500

'To mak an appillinose. Take apples and seethe them and let them cool. Then fret them through sieve. On fish days take almond milk and olive oil thereto. And on flesh days take fresh broth and white grease and sugar and put them in a pot and boil it and colour it with saffron, and cast on powders and serve it.'

APPLE MOYE (3)

Thomas Dawson's *The good Huswifes Handmaide for the Kitchin*, 1594

'To make an Apple Moye. Take apples, and cut them in 2 or 4 pieces. Boil them till they be soft, and bruise them in a mortar. Put thereto the yolks of two eggs, and a little sweet butter. Set them on a chafingdish of charcoal, and boil them a little, and put thereto a little sugar, cinnamon and ginger, and so serve them.'

FRYTURS – APPLE FRITTERS

Gentyll Manly Cokere, MS Pepys 1047, *c.* 1490

For fryturs.

With egges and flowr a bator thow make
Put barme ther to I under take
Collor hit with saferon or thow more do
Take pouder of pepur and cast ther to
Kerve Appyls evyn A thorte cast ther yn
Fry ham in swete grece no more I myn
Cast sugur ther to yf thow be gynne

[With eggs and flour a batter thou makes
Put barm thereto I undertake
Colour it with saffron and thou more do
Take powder of pepper and cast thereto
Carve apples even athwart cast therein
Fry them in sweet grease no more I mind
Cast sugar thereto if thou be gone]

BI-COLOURED CREAM TARTS

Thomas Dawson's *The Second part of The Good Huswifes Jewell*, 1597

'For tartes of cream. Take a pint of cream with 6 raw eggs, and boil them together, and stir it well that it burn not. Then let it boil till it be thick. Then take it out of the pot, and put to two dishes of butter melted, and when it is somewhat cold, then strain it and season it with sugar. Then put it into your pastry, when your pastry is hardened, and when it is cooked, the serve it with sugar cast upon it. If you will have a tart of 2 colours, then take the half of it, when it is in cream, and colour the other half with saffron or yolks of eggs.'

WHITE LEACH

Thomas Dawson's *The Second part of The Good Huswifes Jewell*, 1597

'A white leach. Take a quart of new milk, and three ounces weight of isinglass*, half a pound of beaten sugar, and stir them together. Let it boil half a quarter of an hour till it be thick, stirring all the while. Then strain it with three spoonfuls of rosewater, then put it into a platter and let it cool, and cut it in squares. Lay it fair in dishes, and lay gold upon it.'

*Isinglass was made from the dried swim bladders of sturgeon – a remarkable discovery in itself – and is replaced by gelatine these days. In 1795 William Murdoch invented a cheap substitute for isinglass using cod, but isinglass is still used in fining beers.

WHITE LEACH OF CREAME

A Closet for Ladies and Gentlewomen, 1602

'To make white leach of creame. Take a pint of sweet cream, and six spoonfuls of rosewater, and two grains of musk, two drops of oil of mace, or one piece of large mace. And so let it boile with 4 ounces of isinglass: then let it run down through a jelly bag. When it is cold, slice it like brawn, and so serve it out: this is the best way to make leach.'

LEACH – ELIZABETHAN ALMOND PANNA COTTA

Sir Hugh Plat's *Delightes for Ladies*, 1602

'Seethe a pint of cream, and in the seething put in some dissolved isinglas, stirring it until it be very thick. Then take a handful of blanched almonds, beat them and put them in a dish with your cream, seasoning them with sugar. And after slice it and dish it.'

[Essentially this recipe is the Italian *panna cotta* (cooked cream), enriched with almond paste. Plat's version, however, is set harder than modern panna cottas and is served sliced.]

LEACH OF ALMONDS – ALMOND PUDDING
A Noble Boke off Cookry ffor a Prynce Houssolde Holkham, MSS 674, 1480/1500, and Hugh Plat's *Delights for Ladies*, 1602

'To make Leach of Almonds. Take half a pound of sweet almonds, and beat them in a mortar. Then strain them with a pint of sweet milk from the cow. Then add to it one grain of musk, 2 spoonfuls of rosewater, two ounces of fine sugar, the weight of 3 whole shillings of isinglass that is very white, and so boil them. And let all run through a strainer. Then may you slice the same, and so serve it.'

[A gilded *leche*, *leech* or *leach* was served at Henry VIII's Garter Feast at Windsor in 1520, appearing in both the first and second courses. This rosewater-flavoured jelly featured as a chessboard with the 'black' squares gilded. Leach continued to be a favourite dish at other Garter Feasts until the seventeenth century. Leach was closely related to 'ribband jelly', a jelly moulded in multi-coloured layers (ribbons), also popular in Tudor times.]

LYEDE MILKE – TOASTS IN THIN CUSTARD
Gentyll Manly Cokere, MS Pepys 1047, *c.* 1490

'To make lyede [mixed] milke. Take cow milk and sugar and put them in a pot. Set it on the fire and when it boils add thereto yolks of eggs loke that it be rynnyng [runny?]

and not too charchant [thick]. Take white bread cut in small sops. Put them in dishes and pour it thereupon. And serve it forth.'

ALMOND MILKE

The Good Hous-wiues Treasurie, 1588

'How to make Almond milke. Take a piece of the scrag end of a neck of mutton, a good handful of hulled barley, a good handful of cold herbs* and a litle salt. Then take a handful of almonds & blanch them and grind them in a stone mortar, and strain the liquor through a fair bolter [cloth]. Then put in a little sugar, and so give it to drink.'

*'Hot' conditions were treated with 'cold' herbs such as feverfew, yarrow and chamomile. Cold almond milk could be served over toast for invalids.

20. In this sixteenth-century Belgian engraving, made to showcase new inventions and discoveries of the time, sugar cane is chopped up and put into baskets. From here it is crushed in a watermill, and the pulp brewed into a syrup. The syrup is then crystallised and poured into cones.

MUSKADINE COMFITS

A Closet for Ladies and Gentlewomen, 1608

'To Make Muskadine Comfits. Take half a pound of musk sugar beaten and searsed, then take gum tragacanth, steeped in rosewater, and 2 grains of musk, and so beat them in an alabaster mortar, till it comes to perfect paste. Then drive it very thin with a rolling pin. Then cut it into small pieces like diamonds, some cut with a roll spoon on the sides: being thus cut, store them, and so keep them all the yeare.'

[Musk mallow seeds are the spice component of *Abelmoschus moschatus*, the Annual Hibiscus, and have a sweet, flowery, heavy fragrance similar to that of musk. Today they are most commonly used as a flavouring additive to coffee, but can be used as a flavour base for confectionery, biscuits and cakes as well as some savoury dishes. By late Tudor times, they were being used as a cheaper alternative to animal musk in flavouring spiced wines such as hippocras.]

WALNUT OR GOURD CONFITES (COMFITS, COMFETS)

Thomas Dawson's *The Second part of The Good Huswifes Jewell*, 1597

'To confite walnuts. Take them green and small in husk, and make in them four 4 holes, or more. Then steep them in water 11 days. Make them clean and boil them as ye would oranges here after written, but they must seethe 4 times as much. Dress them likewise with spices, saving you must put in very few cloves, lest they taste bitter. In like sorte you may dress gourds, cutting them in long pieces, and paring away the inner parts.'

POTTAGE OF CHERRIES ON TOAST
A. W.'s *A Book of Cookrye*, 1584 and 1591

'To make pottage of Cherries. Fry white bread in butter till it be brown and so put it into a dish. Then take cherries and take out the stones and fry them where you fried the bread. Then put thereto sugar, ginger and cinnamon. For lack of broth, take white or Claret wine, boil these togither, and that done, serve them upon your toasts.'

RICE POTTAGE
Thomas Dawson's *The good Huswifes Handmaide for the Kitchin*, 1594

'To make fine Rice pottage. Take half a pound of Jordan almonds, and half a pound of rice, and a gallon of running water, and a handful of oak bark, and let the bark be boiled in the running water, and the almonds beaten with the hulls and all on, and so strained to make the rice pottage withall.'

RYSE OF GENOA
Gentyll Manly Cokere, MS Pepys 1047, *c.* 1490

'To make ryse of genoa. Take rice and seethe it in fair water and steep them well. And then take it off and cast in a fair vessel and pyke it clene and set on the fire again. And add thereto broth of fresh beef or of marrowbones and let it seethe well. And add ground saffron & salt and if it be a fasting day temper it with almond milk & serve it forth.'

SIRROPE OF VIOLETS

Thomas Dawson's *The Second part of The Good Huswifes Jewell*, 1597

'To make sirrope of Violets. First gather a great quantity of violet flowers, and pick them clean from the stalks and set them on the fire, and put to them so much rosewater as you thinke good. Then let them boil altogether until the colour be out of them. Then take them off the fire and strain them through a fine cloth, then put so much sugar to them as you think good, then set it again to the fire until it be somewhat thick, and put it into a violet glass.'

TARTE OWTE OF LENT – TUDOR CREAM CHEESE COFFIN

Gentyll Manly Cokere, MS Pepys 1047, *c.* 1490

'Tarte owt of Lent. Take neshe [soft] cheese and pare it and grind it in a mortar and break eggs and add. And then put in butter and cream and meld all well together. Add not too much butter therein, if the cheese be fat. Make a coffin of dough and close it above with dough, and colour it above with the yolks of eggs. Bake it well and serve it forth.'

LUMBARDY TARTES

Thomas Dawson's *The good Huswifes Handmaide for the Kitchin*, 1594

'To make Lumbardy tartes. Take beets, chop them small, and add to them grated bread and cheese, and mingle them well in the chopping. Take a few currants, and a dish of sweet butter, & melt it. Then stir all these in the butter, together with three yolks of eggs, cinnamon, ginger and sugar, and make your tart as large as you will. Fill it with the stuff, bake it, and serve it.'

TARTE OF BREAD
Thomas Dawson's *The good Huswifes Handmaide for the Kitchin*, 1594
'To make a tarte of bread. Take grated bread, and add to it molten butter, and a little rosewater and sugar, and the yolks of eggs. Put it into your paste, and bake, and when you serve it, cut it in four quarters and cast sugar on it.'

PRESERVED ORRENGE CANDY
Thomas Dawson's *The Second part of The Good Huswifes Jewell*, 1597
'To preserve orrenges. Take your peels and water them two nights & one day, and dry them clean again and boil them over a soft fire the space of one hour. Then take them out to cool, and make your syrup half with rosewater and half with that liquor, and put double sugar to your oranges, and when your syrup is half sodden, then let your oranges seethe one quarter of an hour more. Then take out your oranges and let the syrup seethe until it rope [unsure of this meaning], and when all is cold, then put your oranges into the syrup. The white of an egg and sugar beaten together will make it to candy.'

APPLE FRITTERS
Thomas Dawson's *The good Huswifes Handmaide for the Kitchin*, 1594
'To make Fritters. Take a pint of ale, and four yolks of eggs, and a fair little saffron, a spoonful of cloves and

mace, and a little salt, and a half a handful of sugar. Put all this in a fair platter, and stir them all together with a spoon, and make your batter thereof. Then take 10 apples, pare and cut them as big as a groat, put them in your batter. Then take your suet & set it on the fire, & when it is hot, add your batter & your apples to your suet with your hand one by one. When they be fair and yellow, take them out, and lay them in a fair platter, and let them stand a little while by the fireside. Then take a fair platter, and lay your fritters therein, and cast a little sugar on them, and so serve them.'

MANUS CHRISTI (1)

A Closet for Ladies and Gentlewomen, 1602

'To make Manus Christi. Take half a pound of refined sugar, and some rosewater, and boil them together, till it come to sugar again, then stir it about while it be somewhat cold. Then take your gold leaf, and mingle with it, then cast it according to art, that is, in round gobbets, and so keep them.'

MANUS CHRISTI (2)

Thomas Dawson's *The Good Huswifes Jewell*, 1596

'To make Manus Christi. Take 6 spoonefuls of rosewater, and grains of ambergris, and 4 grains of pearl beaten very fine. Put these three together in a saucer and cover it close, and let it stand covered one hour. Then take 4 ounces of very fine sugar, and beat it small, and sieve it through a fine sieve. Then take a little earthenware pot glazed, and put into it a spoonful of sugar, and a quarter of spoonful of rosewater. Let the sugar and the rosewater boil together softly, till it do rise and fall again three times. Then take fine rye flour, and sift on a smooth board, and with a spoon take of the sugar, and the rosewater, and first make it all into a round cake, and then after into little cakes. And when they be half colde, wet them over with the same rosewater, and then lay on your gold, and so shall you make very good Manus Christi [the Hand of Christ].'

MANUS CHRISTI (3)

John Partridge's *The Treasurie of commodious Conceits*, 1573

'To Make MANVS CHRISTI. Take half a pound of white sugar, add thereto 4 ounces of rosewater. Seethe them upon a soft fire of charcoal, till the water be consumed, and the sugar is become hard. Then put therein a quarter of an ounce of the powder of pearls. Stir them well together, add for every spoonful a piece of a leaf of gold cut for that purpose. Cast them upon a leaf of white paper, annointed first, with the oil of sweet almonds, or sweet butter, for cleaving to.'

TO PURIFY HONEY FOR CONFITS

Thomas Dawson's *The Second part of The Good Huswifes Jewell*, 1597

'How to purifie and prepare Honnye and Sugar for to confite citrons and all other fruites. Take every time 10 pound of honey, the white of 12 new laid eggs, and take away the froth of them. Beat them well together with a stick, and 6 glasses of fair fresh water. Then put them into the honey, and boil them in a pot with a moderate fire the space of a quarter of an hour or less, then take them from the fire skimming them well.'

TARTE OF ALMONDS

Thomas Dawson's *The good Huswifes Handmaide for the Kitchin*, 1594

'To make a tarte of Almonds. Blanch almonds and beat them, and strain them &c, with good thick cream. Then add in sugar and rosewater, and boil it thick. Then make your pastry with butter, fair water, and the yolks of 2 or 3 eggs, and as soon as you have rolled your pastry, cast on a little sugar and rosewater, and harden your pastry afore in the oven. Then take it out, and fill it, and set it in again, and let it bake till it be well, and so serve it.'

ORANGE PEEL CONFITS

Thomas Dawson's *The Second part of The Good Huswifes Jewell*, 1597

'To confite Orange peels which may be doone at all times in the yeere, and cheefly in May, because then the saide peels be greatest and thickest. Take thick orange peels, and them cut in 4 or 5 pieces, and steep them in water the space of 10 or 12 days. You may know when they be steeped enough, if you hold them up in the sun and see through them, then they be steeped enough. If you cannot see through them, then let them steep until you may. Then lay them to dry upon a table, and put them to dry between two linen clothes. Then put them in a kettle or leaded vessel, and add to it as much honey as will half cover the said peels, more or less as you think good. Boil them a little and stir them always, then take them from the fire, least the honey should seethe overmuch. For if it should boil a little more than it ought to boil, it would be thick. Let it then stand and rest 4 days in the said honey, stirring and mingling the orange and honey every day together. Because there is not honey enough to cover all the said orange peels, you must stir them well and oftentimes, thus do 3 times, giving them one bobbling at ech time. Then let them stand 3 days then strain them from the honey, and after you have let them boil a small space, take them from the fire, and bestow them in vessels, adding to them ginger, cloves and cinnamon. Mix all together, and the rest of the syrup will serve to dress others withall.'

ROCK CANDIED GINGER
A Closet for Ladies and Gentlewomen, 1602

'To Candy Ginger. Take very fair and large ginger, and pare it, and then lay it in water a day and a night. Then take your double refined sugar, and boil it to the height of sugar again. Then when your sugar beginneth to be cold, take your ginger, and stir it well about while your sugar is hard to the pan. Then take it out root by root, and lay it by the fire for 4 hours. Then take a pot and warm it, and put the ginger in it. Then tie it very close, & every second morning stir it about roundly, and it will be rock candied in a very short space.'

BUTTER BIKKIES
Thomas Dawson's *The Good Huswifes Jewell*, 1596

'To make a butter paste. Take flour, and 7 or 8 eggs, and cold butter & fair water, or rosewater, and spices (if you will). Make your pastry and beat it on a board, and when you have so done, divide it into 2 or 3 parts. Roll out the piece with a rolling pin, and dab with butter one piece by another, and then fold up your pastry upon the butter and drive it out again. And so do 5 or 6 times together, and some not cut for bearings, and put them into the oven, and when they be baked, scrape sugar on them, and serve them.'

CANDIED ROSE LEAVES
A Closet for Ladies and Gentlewomen, 1602
'To Candy Rose leaves as naturally as if they grew upon the Tree. Take of the fairest rose leaves, red or damask, and on a sunshine day sprinkle them with rosewater. Lay them one by one upon fair paper, then take some double refined sugar, and beat it very fine, and put it in a fine linen sieve. When you have laid abroad all the rose leaves in the hottest of the sun, sieve sugar thinly all over them, then anon the Sun will candy the sugar. Then turne the leaves, and sieve sugar on the other side. Turn them often in the Sun, sometimes sprinkling rosewater, & some times sieving sugar on them, until they be enough, and come to your liking. And being thus done, you may keep them.'

CANDIED MARIGOLDS AFTER THE SPANISH FASHION
A Closet for Ladies and Gentlewomen, 1602
'To Candy Marigolds in wedges the Spanish fashion. Take of the fair yellow marigold flowers, two ounces, and shred them, and dry them before the fire. Then take four ounces of sugar, and boil it to the height of Manus Christi, then pour it upon a wet pie plate, and betwixt hot and cold, cut it into wedges. Then lay them on a sheet of white paper, and put them in a stove.'

SUGAR-CANDIED FLOWERS
A Closet for Ladies and Gentlewomen, 1602

'To Candy all manner of flowers in their naturall colours. Take the flowers with the stalks, and wash them over with a little rosewater, wherein gum-arabic is dissolved. Then take fine sieved sugar, and dust over them, and set them drying on the bottom of a sieve in an oven, and they will glister as if it were sugar-candy.'

PEACH CONFITS AFTER THE FRENCH FASHION
Thomas Dawson's *The Second part of The Good Huswifes Jewell*, 1597

'To confite Peaches after the Spanish fashion. Take great and fair peaches and peel them clean. Cut them in pieces and so lay them upon a table abroad in the Sun the space of two days, turning them everye morning and night. Put them hot into a julep of sugar syrup, and prepared as is aforesaid. And after you have taken them out set them again in the Sun, turning them often untill they be well dried. This done, put them again into the julep, then set them in the sun until they have gotten a fair bark or crust. Then you may keep them in boxes for winter.'

ICED MARCHPANE – STIFF MARZIPAN
A Closet for Ladies and Gentlewomen, 1602

'To make a Marchpane, to yce it, and garnish it after the Art of Comfit making. Take two pound of small almonds blanched, and beaten into perfect paste, with a pound of sugar finely sieved, putting in now and then a spoonful or two of rosewater, to keep it from oiling. And when it is beaten to perfect paste, roll it thin, and cut it round by a charger, then set an edge on it, as you do on a tart.

Then dry it in an oven, or a backing pan, then ice it with rosewater and sugar, made as thick as batter for fritters. When it is iced garnish it with conceits, and stick long comfits in it, and so gild it, and serve it.'

MARZIPAN BANQUETING TRIFLES, 'EXCELLENT GOOD TO PLEASE CHILDREN'

A Closet for Ladies and Gentlewomen, 1602

'To make all sorts of banqueting conceits of Marchpane stuffe, some like Pyes, Birds, Baskets, and such like, and some to print with moulds. Take a pound of almond paste, made for the marchpane, and dry it on a chafingdish of charcoal, till you see it wax white. Then you may print some with moulds, and make some with hands, and so gild them, then store them and you may keepe them all the year. They be excellent good to please children.'

TART OF CREAM

Thomas Dawson's *The good Huswifes Handmaide for the Kitchin*, 1594

'To make a good Tart of Cream. Take a quart of cream, and put in 12 yolks of eggs, and a little saffron, and strain them. Then put it in a pot and boil it, but all the time it standeth on the fire it must be stirred with a stick for burning. Also ere ye boil it, ye must put a good dish of butter in it. When it is boiled, put in your sugar, as much as will make it sweet. Then make your pastry with butter, eggs, sugar, with a little saffron and fine flour, and make your tart with it, and dry it in the oven. When it is dry, put in a little rosewater and butter, then fill your tart with the stuff. When it is strained, so bake it, and when it is baked, sprinkle a little rosewater and sugar, and a little butter molten upon it.'

ROCKE CANDY
A Closet for Ladies and Gentlewomen, 1602
'To Candy all sorts of flowers, fruits, and spices, the cleare rocke Candy. Take two pound of Barbary sugar,* great grained, clarified with the whites of two eggs, and bol it almost as high as for Manus Christi. Then put it into a pipkin, that is, not very rough, then put in your flowers, fruits and spices, and so put your pipkin into a still, and make a small fire of small charcoal under it, and in the space of twelve days, it will be rock candied.'
*When Islamic armies conquered Persia, they found sugar cane and adopted its cultivation, carrying it with them in their conquests, calling it 'the Persian Reed'. Sugar cane was introduced to Egypt after their defeat by the Arabs in 710 CE, and Egyptians developed clarification, crystallisation and refining processes. Sugar cane production passed across Northern Africa reaching Morocco and the Barbary Coast. It reached Southern Spain by 755 and Sicily in 950. Production of sugar then was a primitive process. A blindfolded mule or ox treading in a circle, drove a vertical grinding mill or a pestle in a mortar to crush the cane, and the juice was evaporated by boiling to a sticky mixture of crystals and syrup. In the Middle Ages similar equipment was used to produce sugar, and in Sicily the grinding stone was powered usually by men. A contemporary description says that going into the place was like entering the Forge of Vulcan, 'the men who worked there being blackened by the smoke from the fires, dirty, sweaty, and scorched, more like demons than men'. In tenth-century Europe, sugar was considered a valuable medicine. Later, it was

considered a rare spice and its price was as high as that of pepper, saffron and cinnamon. Like those spices, the Arabs also controlled the European sugar trade.

Because of its exalted prestige, sugar was used to season things to a degree that today we would consider excessive, thus meats were often cooked in a heavy syrup of sugar with almonds and fruit. Shipping and trade between the Middle East, North Africa and Europe was almost exclusively in the hands of Venetian merchants. Special jars of rose and violet sugars, flavoured with aromatic substances and extremely expensive, were made for sickly royal children. Sugar was so rare that a teaspoon of it in Tudor times cost around £3, and in the seventeenth century one could purchase a calf for four pounds of sugar. In the early Tudor era the best sugar came from Morocco, and by the mid-sixteenth century much of the sugar consumed in England was bought from 'Barbary', now called Morocco. However, towards the end of the Tudor era it began coming in from the slave plantations of the Americas.

CANDIED VIOLET FLOWERS

A Closet for Ladies and Gentlewomen, 1602

'To Candy Violet flowers. Take your violet flowers which are good and new, and well coloured, and weigh them. To every ounce of your violet flowers, you must take 4 ounces of refined sugar, which is very white and fair grained, and dissolve it in 2 ounces of fair running water. And so boil it till it come to sugar again, but you must skim it often, least it be not clear enough. When it is boiled to sugar again, take it off and let it cool. Then put in your violet flowers, stirring them together till the sugar grows hard to the pan. This done, put them into a box, and keep them in a stove.'

CANDIED GOOS-BERRIES

A Closet for Ladies and Gentlewomen, 1602

'To Candy Goos-berries. Take your fairest berries, but they must not be too ripe, for then they will not be so good, and with a linen cloth wipe them very clean. And pick off all the stalks from them, and weigh them. To every ounce of berries, you must take 2 ounces of sugar, and half an ounce of sugarcandy. And dissolve them in an ounce or two of rosewater, & so boil them up to the height of Manus Christi. When it is come to its perfect height, let it cool and put in your berries, for if you put them in hot, they will shrink, and so stir them round with a wooden spatter [spatula], till they be candied. And thus put them up and keep them.'

CANDIED ROSEMARY FLOWERS

A Closet for Ladies and Gentlewomen, 1602

'To Candy Rosemarie flowers. Take your rosemarie flowers, ready picked, and weigh them. To every ounce of flowers, you must take 2 ounces of hard sugar, and 1 ounce of sugar-candy, and dissolve them in rosemary flower water. Boil them till they come to sugar again. Which done, put in your rosemary flowers. When your sugar is almost cold, so stir them together, until they be ready. Then take them out, and put them in a box, and keep them for your use in your stove.'

WHITE AND YELLOW BLEWMANGER ROLLS

Thomas Dawson's *The Good Huswifes Jewell*, 1596

'To make Blewmanger. Take to a pint of cream 12 or 16 yolks of eggs, and strain them into it. Seethe them well, always stirring with a stick that is broad at the end, but before you seethe it put in sugar. And in the seething, taste of it, for you may need to put in more sugar. When it is almost sodden put in a little rosewater that it may taste thereof, and seethe it well till it be thick. Then strain it again if it hath need, or else put it in a faire dish and stir it till it be almost cold. And take the white of all the 12 or 16 eggs, and strain them with a pint of Cream and seethe that with sugar, and in the end put in rosewater as into the other, and seethe it till it be thick enough, and then use it as the other. And when ye serve it, ye may serve one dish and another of the other in rolls, and cast on biskets.'

LENTON PUDDING
The Good Hous-wiues Treasurie, 1588
'How to make a Lenton Pudding [for Lent]. Take grated bread, a little sugar, nutmegs, cinnamon, salt, and yolks of eggs, tempered with a litle cream.'

CAUDLE
Thomas Dawson's *The Second part of The Good Huswifes Jewell*, 1597
'To make a caudle. Take a pint of Malmsey and 5 or 6 eggs, and seethe them strained together, till ready. Stir it till it be thick, and lay it in a dish as you do please, and so serve it.'

OLD MAN'S CAUDLE
Thomas Dawson's *The Good Huswifes Jewell*, 1596
'To make a Caudle to comfort the stomacke, good for an old man. Take a pint of good Muscadine [a sweet wine], and as much of good stale ale, mingle them together. Then

take the yolks of 12 or 13 eggs newly laid. Beat well the eggs first by themselves, with the wine and ale, and so boil together. Put thereto a quartern [¼ pint] of sugar, and a few whole mace, and so stir it well, till it seethes a good while. When it is well sodden [cooked], put therein a few slices of bread if you will. And so let it soak a while, and it will be right good and wholesome.'

GODE ALMONDYS MYLKE
Gentyll Manly Cokere, MS Pepys 1047, *c*. 1490
'To make gode almondys mylke. Take broken sugar or if you have none, take clarified honey and put it into fair water. And set it on the fire and boil it and skim it clean. And set it beside the fire and let it cool and then blanch thy almonds. Cast them in a morter and bray them small, and temper them up with the same water.'

DOWCETTS (1) – SMALL TARTS OF MARROW, SPICES AND ALMOND MILK
Gentyll Manly Cokere, MS Pepys 1047, *c*. 1490
'Dowcetts. Take pastry and make little coffins smaller than saucers. Set them in the oven and harden them and take marrow of an ox and good almond milk [see above]. Stir them well together with sugar, powder of ginger, cinnamon and salt and put in the coffin. Set them in the oven to bake and serve forth all with white colours.'

DOUSETS (2)
The Good Hous-wiues Treasurie, 1588
'How to make Dousets. Take a pint of flour. Wet it with water, butter, an egg white and all, and make not your

pastry too light. When they be raised, prick them with a pin on the bottom, then harden them either on the hearth or in the oven. Take a pint of cream, 3 eggs, but one of the whites, beat them well and mingle them with the cream. Then take cinnamon, nutmeg, sugar, and a little salt, and a quarter of a spoonful of flour. Stir them all together & strain them through a boulter or strainer, then fill them in the oven. Let them stand in half an hour and then take them out.'

SNOW (1)

A Closet for Ladies and Gentlewomen, 1602

'To make Snow. Take the whites of 5 or 6 eggs, a handful of fine sugar, and as much rosewater. Put them in a pottle [4 pints] of cream of the thickest that you can get. Beat them all together. As the snow rises, take it off with a spoon. You must beat it with a stick cloven in four [a Tudor 'whisk']. Then must you take a loaf of bread and cut away the crust, and set it upright in a platter. Then set a fair rosemary branch in the loaf, and cast your snow upon it with a spoon.'

SNOWE (2)

Thomas Dawson's *The good Huswifes Handmaide for the Kitchin*, 1594

'To make Snowe. Take a quart of thick cream, and 5 or 6 whites of eggs, a saucerful of sugar, and a saucerful of rosewater. Beat all together, and ever as it riseth take it out with a spoon. Then take a loaf of bread, cut away the crust, and set it upright in a platter. Then set a fair great rosemary bush in the midst of your bread. Then lay your snow with a spoon upon your rosemary, & upon your bread, & gild it.'

A DISHEFULL OF SNOW (3)
A Proper New Booke of Cookery, 1545 and 1575
'To make a dishefull of Snow. Take a pottle of sweet thick cream and the white of 8 eggs, and beat them altogether with a spoon. Then put them in your cream, and a saucer full of rosewater, and a dishful of sugar withall. Then take a stick and make it clean, and then cut it in the end four square. Therewith beat all the aforesaid things together. And ever as it riseth, take it off, and put it into a colander. This done, take an apple and set it in the midst of it, and a thick bush of rosemary. And set it in the midst of the platter, then cast your snow upon the rosemary, and fll your platter therewith. And if you have wafers, cast some in withall, & thus serve them forth.'

CUSTARD
Thomas Dawson's *The Good Huswifes Jewell*, 1596
'To make a Custard. Break your eggs into a bowl, and put your cream into another bowl, and strain your eggs into the cream. Put in saffron, cloves and mace, and a little cinnamon and ginger, and if you will some sugar and butter. Season it with salt, and melt your butter, and stir it with the ladle a good while, and dub your custard with dates or currants.'

ALMOND CUSTARD
Thomas Dawson's *The Second part of The Good Huswifes Jewell*, 1597
'To make an Almond Custard. Take a good sort of almonds blanched, and stamp them with water, and strain them with water and a little rosewater, and 12 eggs. Then season it with a little cinnamon, sugar, and a good deal of ginger. Then set it upon a pot of seething water, & when it is enough [ready] stick dates in it.'

A GOOD CUSTARD
Thomas Dawson's *The good Huswifes Handmaide for the Kitchin*, 1594
'To make a good Custard. Take a platter full of cream. If it be a quart, then take 6 yolks of eggs, to a pint 3 eggs. When you set your cream, over the fire, cut your butter in small pieces and put it into your cream, & it be little more than the quantity of a walnut it is enough. Season it with salt, sugar, cloves, mace and saffron, and so cover it. Let it be set upon a chafingdish or pot of seething water, and when it is well hardened, cast on it minced dates and small raisins. And so let it boil till ye think it be well hardened: and then serve forth.'

CUSTARD IN A COFFIN – CUSTARD PIE
A Proper New Booke of Cookery, 1545 and 1575
'To make a Custarde. The coffin must be first hardened in the oven, and then take a quart of cream, and 5 or 6 yolks of eggs, and beat them well together. And put them into the cream, and put in sugar & small raisins and dates, and put into the coffin butter, or else marrow, but on the fish days put in butter.'

CUSTARD IN LENT
Thomas Dawson's *The good Huswifes Handmaide for the Kitchin*, 1594
'How to make a Custard in Lent. Take the milt of any manner of fresh fish, and a little of the milt of a white herring, and a quantity of blanched almonds, and crumbs of bread, and mingle all these together. Add a little water and sugar, and a quantity of rosewater, and mingle together. Season it as ye would do another custard with all manner of spices. Then mingle therewith raisins, currants and dates cut in pieces, and so bake it in a platter or pastry, whether ye will, the space of half an hour, and so serve it.'

QUODINIACKE OF PLUMS
A Closet for Ladies and Gentlewomen, 1602
'To make Quodiniacke of plums. Take two pounds of plums, and put them into a posnet with a pound and half of Brazil sugar, clarified with a pint of fair water. Let it boil till the plums break, then take it off, and let your liquid substance run through a strainer. Then put it again into the posnet, and so let it boil till it comes to a thickness, and then print it with your moulds on what fashion you please.'

CONDONACK
Thomas Dawson's *The Second part of The Good Huswifes Jewell*, 1597
'To make a condonack. Take quinces and pare them, take out the cores, and seethe them in fair water until they break. Then strain them through a fine strainer. For 8 pounds of the said strained quinces, you must put in 3 pounds of sugar, and mingle it together in a vessel.

Boil them in the fire, always stirring it until it be sodden, which you may perceive, for it will no longer cleave to the vessel. You may add musk in powder, you may also add spice to it, such as ginger, cinnamon, cloves and nutmegs, as much as you think meet, boiling the musk with a little vinegar. Then with a broad slice of wood spread this confection upon a table, which must be first strewed with sugar, and there make what proportion you will. And set it in the sun until it be dry, and when it hath stood a while turn it upsidown, making always a bed of sugar, both under and above. And turn them still, and dry them in the sun untill they have gotten a crust. In like manner you may dresse pears, peaches, damsons, and other fruits.'

A FINE CRYSTAL JELLY
A Closet for Ladies and Gentlewomen, 1602

'To make fine Christall Gelly. Take a knuckle of veal, and foure calves' feet, and set them on the fire with a gallon of fair water. When the flesh is boiled tender, take it out, then let the liquor stand still until it be cold. Then take away the top and the bottom of that liquor, and put the rest into a clean pipkin. Add into it one pound of clarified sugar, 4 or 5 drops of oil of cinnamon and nutmegs, a grain of musk, and so let it boil a quarter of an hour leisurely on the fire. Then let it run through a jelly bag into a basin with the whites of two eggs beaten. When it is cold, you may cut it into lumps with a spoon, and so serve three or four lumps upon a plate.'

MOCK WALNUT FORTUNE COOKIES
A Closet for Ladies and Gentlewomen, 1602

'To make a Walnut, that when you cracke it, you shall find Biskets, and Carrawayes in it, or a prettie Posey written. Take a piece of your white royal pastry*, being beaten with gum tragacanth, and mixed with a little fine sieved cinnamon, which will bring your pastry into a walnut-shell colour. Then roll it thin, and cut it into two pieces, and put the one piece into the one half of your mould, and the other into the other, then put what you please into the nut, and close the mould together, & so make three or four walnuts.'

The Proper Newe Booke of Cookerye, c. 1557, gives a recipe for 'paest royall', the richest pastry of the age for pies and desserts. As the flour is very fine, this would only have been used for the very best tables: 'To make Pyes ... And if you will have paest royall / take butter and yolkes of egges & so to temper the floure to make the paest.'

BISKATELLO – SUGAR BISCUITS
A Closet for Ladies and Gentlewomen, 1602

'To make Biskatello. Take two ounces of very fine sugar, beaten and sieved, and put into it half a spoonful of Amidum, that is, white starch, and a grain of Musk. Then beat it into perfect pastry with gum tragacanth steeped in rosewater. Then make it into little pretty loaves, after the fashion of manchets, and so put a wafer in the bottom of every one of them. Bake them in a baking-pan, but take heed your pan be not hot, and so speck them with gold, and so box them. It is a very fine banqueting conceit.'

TRIFLE
Thomas Dawson's *The Good Huswifes Jewell*, 1596
'To make a Trifle. Take a pint of thick cream, and season it with sugar, ginger and rosewater. So stir it as you would then have it, and make it luke warm in a dish on a chafingdishe of charcoal. And after put it into a silver piece or a bowl, and so serve it to the board [table].'
[Only the extremely rich had silver tableware.]

PANCAKES
Thomas Dawson's *The good Huswifes Handmaide for the Kitchin*, 1594
'To make Pancakes. Take a pint of new thick cream, 4 or 5 yolks of eggs, a good handful of flour, and 2 or 3 spoonfuls of ale. Strain them all together into a fair platter, and season it with a good handful of sugar, a spoonful of cinnamon, and a little ginger. Then take a frying pan, and put in a little piece of butter, as big as your thumb. And when it is molten brown, cast it out of your pan, and with a ladle put to the further side of your pan some of your mixture, and hold your pan aslope, so that your stuff may run abroad over all the pan, as thin as may be. Then set it to the fire, and let the fire be very soft, and when the one side is baked, then turn the other, and bake them as dry as ye can without burning.'
[The addition of ale works well.]

100 JUMBLES
Thomas Dawson's *The Second part of The Good Huswifes Jewell*, 1597
'To make Iombils a hundred. Take 20 eggs and put them into a pot, both the yolks & the white. Beat them well,

then take a pound of beaten sugar and add to them, and stir them well together. Then add to it a quarter of a peck of flower, and make a hard pastry thereof. And then with aniseed, mould it well, and make it in little rolls being long, and tie them in knots. Wet the ends in rosewater, then put them into a pan of seething water, but in one warm. Then take them out with a skimmer and lay them in a cloth to dry. This being done lay them in a tart pan, the bottom being oiled, then put them into a temperate oven for one hour, turning them often in the oven.'

SWEET LOZENGES

John Partridge's *The Treasurie of commodious Conceits*, 1573

'To make Losings. Take half a pound of sugar, and as much rosewater: or other distilled water, as for Manus Christi. Seethe them likewise, and when ye will know when it is sodden through, take out some upon a knife's point, and let it cool. If it be hard like sugar, then it is sodden enough. Then put into it of any of the powders hereafter next following, one ounce. Stir them well together, lay it upon a paper oiled. Roll it as thin as ye think meet, lay on your golde leaf with a using a rabbit's tail as a brush. Cut your lozenges diamond fashion, and so keep them.'

A TARTE OF RYCE

Thomas Dawson's *The Good Huswifes Jewell*, 1596

'To make a Tarte of Ryce. Boyle your rice, and put in the yolks of two or three eggs into the rice. When it is boyled, put it into a dish, and season it with sugar, cinnamon, ginger and butter, and the juice of two or three oranges, and set it on the fire again.'

GENOA PEACH AND QUINCE SWEETS
A Closet for Ladies and Gentlewomen, 1602
'To make Past of Genua the true way. Take two pounds of the pulp of quinces, and as much of peaches, and strain it. Dry it in a pewter platter upon a chafingdish of charcoals, then weigh it, and take as much sugar as it weighs, and boil it to the height of Manus Christi. And then add them together, and so fashion it upon a pie plate, and dry it in an oven with a chafingdish of charcoal, until it be throrough drie. And then if it pleases you, you may spot them with gold.'

VIOLET SWEETS AS A BANQUETING CONCEIT
A Closet for Ladies and Gentlewomen, 1602
'To make Past of Violets. You must take your Violets, which are ready picked, & bruise them in an alabaster or marble mortar and wring the juice from them into a porringer. And put as much hard sugar in fine powder as that juice will cover. Dry it, and then powder it again, and then take as much gum tragacanth steeped in rose water, as will bring this sugar into a perfect paset. When it is perfect, take it up and print it with your moulds, and so dry it in your stove, and not by the fire for fear of danger. And when it is dry, gild it. It is a fine banqueting conceit.'

ROYALL WHITE SUGAR SWEETS
A Closet for Ladies and Gentlewomen, 1602

'To make Past Royall white. Take a pound of refined sugar beaten and sieved, and put into an alabaster mortar, with an ounce of gum tragacanth, steeped in rosewater. And if you see your paste be too weak, add in more sugar, if too dry, more gum, with a drop or two of oil of cinnamon, so that you never deceive yourself to stand upon quantities. Beat it into perfect paste, and then you may print it with your moulds, and when dry, gild, and so keep them.'

ROYAL SPICE SUGAR SWEETS
A Closet for Ladies and Gentlewomen, 1602

'To make Past royall in spices. Take cinnamon and ginger, of each a like quantity, being finely sieved, and mingle it with your sieved sugar, and gum tragacanth steeped in rosewater. Worke it into paste, as you did your Past royall white [above recipe], and then you may turn it upon sticks made of pieces of arrows, and make them hollow like cinnamon sticks. In like manner you may make it taste of what spices you please.'

VERY SWEETE CAKES OF DAMASKE OR RED ROSES
The Good Hous-wiues Treasurie, 1588

'How to make very sweete Cakes either of Damaske or red Roses. Take your roses very fair coloured and somewhat close. If you will make your cakes large take a peck of roses to every cake, or half a peck. Put two cakes together bottom to bottom, and put into every cake besides two handfuls of sweet marjoram, roots and all, for at that time of the year cut marjoram is not sweet. Cut off the roots of sweet marjoram, and two good handfuls of lavender and an ounce of the best Damaske powder you can get, a quarter of a pound of orris and one ounce of cloves. Let not the cloves or the orris be beaten much. When you do sieve your orris see it be not worm-eaten and smell well. All this powder will serve but for 4 cakes. Strew into your still some roses first in the bottom, then marjoram, lavender, and some powder and then roses again and a little powder, then lavender and marjoram, more powder then you did before, then put a few roses in the top somewhat thin. When they be half stilled take them forth and lay them betwixt two papers and lay not one cake against another before they be cold. Then save them in papers, and cut the papers bigger then the cakes, and sew them round as soon as you can put them into an oven after they be stilled. And heat the oven no hotter than if it were after pies or cakes, and let them stay no longer than a day or a night. Then take them out and when they be cold lay them betwixt your clothes, and if they be not dry then set them in again a weeke or a fortnight, and after they be through dry. Prick the papers on both sides unto the brim everywhere thick, these cakes will continue three or four years.'

GENOA (OR GENEVA) APPLE SWEETS
A Closet for Ladies and Gentlewomen, 1602

'To make Past of Pippins the GENVA fashion, some with leaves, some like Plums with staulkes, and stones in them. Take your pippins, and pare them, and cut them in quarters, then boil them in fair water till they be tender. Then strain them, and dry the pulp upon a chafingdish of charcoal, then weigh it. And take as much sugar as it weighs, and boil it to [the height of] Manus Christi, and put them together. Then fashion them upon a pie plate, and put it into an oven, being very slightly heated. The next morning you may turn it, and put them off the plates upon sheets of paper upon a hurdle, and so put them into an oven of like heat. There let them remain 4 or 5 dayes, putting every day a chafingdish of charcoal into the oven, and when they be thoroughly dry, you may box them, and keep them all the year.'

9

Bread, Pastry, Biscuits and Cakes

BISKET BREAD
Thomas Dawson's *The Good Huswifes Jewell*, 1596
'To make Bisket bread. First take half a peck of fine white flour, also 8 new laid eggs, the whites and yolks beaten together. Then put the said eggs into the flour. Then take 8 graines of fine musk, and stamp it in a mortar. Then add half a pint of good damask water, or else rosewater into the musk, and mingle it together, and put it into wine or muskadine* but muskadine is better. Add it into the flour, also one ounce of good aniseeds, clean picked and added therein, and so work them altogether into a pastry, as ye doe bread. And then make your biskettes into what fashion you think best, and then put them into an oven, and bake them hard if you will keep them long, or else but indifferent. If you will have it candied, take rosewater and sugar, and boil them together till they be thick, and so slices of bread, then set hot in the oven until the same be candied.'
*Today this is sweet red wine from the muscadine grape.

FINE BISKET BREAD
Thomas Dawson's *The Good Huswifes Jewell*, 1596
'To make fine bisket bread. Take a pound of fine flour, and a pound of sugar, and mingle it together, with a quarter of a pound of aniseeds, 4 eggs, and 2 or 3 spoonfuls of rosewater. Put all these into an earthenware pan. And with a slice of wood beat it the space of two houres. Then fill your moulds half full. Your moulds must be of tin, and then let it into the oven, your oven being so hot as it were for cheat bread*. Let it stand one houre and a half. Your must annoint your moulds with butter before you put it your mixture, and when you will occupy of it, slice it thin and dry it in the oven, your oven being no hotter than you may abide your hand in the bottom.'

*In Tudor and medieval times, this was wholewheat bread with the coarse bran removed.

PRINCE BISKET BREAD
A Closet for Ladies and Gentlewomen, 1602
'To make Prince bisket bread. Take a pound of very fine flour, as much sugar throughly sieved, one ounce of aniseeds cleane picked. Take 8 eggs and a spoonful of Muskadine, and beat all into batter as thick as for fritters. Beat it thus in a bowl for one hour, then put it into your coffins of plate, or frames of wood, and set in an oven. Let it remain there one hour. You may slice some of them when they be a day old, and dry them again upon a hurdle of wicker. You may also take one of your loaves, and wash it over with the yolk of an egg, beaten with a little rose water, and while it is green, cast biskets and caraways on it and a little white candy, and it will show as if it did hail on it, then spot it with gold and give to whom you please.'

ROSE WATER BISCUITS

Thomas Dawson's *The Good Huswifes Jewell*, 1596

'To make fine Cakes. Take fine flour and good Damask rose water. You must have no other liquor but that. Then take sweet butter, two or three yolks of eggs and a good quantity of sugar, and a few cloves, and mace, as your cook's mouth shall serve you, and a little saffron, and a little God's good* about a spoonful. If you put in too much they shall arise. Cut them in squares like unto trenchers, and prick them well, and let your oven be well swept and lay them upon papers. So set them into the oven. Do not burn them. If they be three or four days old they be the better.'

*The *Godecookery* website places this as hartshorn. Hartshorn is the horn of a male red deer, and various substances were made from hartshorn shavings. Oil of hartshorn is an animal oil obtained from the distillation of the deers' bones or horns. Salt of hartshorn refers ammonium carbonate, an early form of smelling salts, obtained by dry distillation of oil of hartshorn. Hartshorn salt (ammonium carbonate), also known simply as hartshorn or 'baker's ammonia', was used as a leavening agent in the baking of biscuits and other edible treats, a forerunner of baking powder. A half-teaspoon of hartshorn equals a teaspoon of baking powder, but hartshorn may still be purchased as a baking ingredient. Biscuits made with hartshorn can be kept for a long time without hardening, and it is especially suited to thin, dry biscuits and crackers.

SHORT CAKES

Thomas Dawson's *The good Huswifes Handmaide for the Kitchin*, 1594

'To make short Cakes. Take wheat flour, the fairest ye can get, and put it in an earthenware pot. Stop it close, and set it in an oven and bake it, and when it is baked, it will be full of clods. Therefore ye must sieve it through a sieve. The flour will have as long baking as a pasty of venison. When you have done this, take clotted cream, or else sweet butter, but cream is better. Then take sugar, cloves, mace and saffron, and the yolk of an egg. For one dozen cakes, one yolk is enough. Then put all these aforesaid things together into the cream, & temper them all together. Then add them to your flour and so make your cakes. Your pastry wil be very short, therefore ye must make your cakes very little. When ye bake your cakes, ye must bake them upon papers, after the drawing of a batch of bread.'

A TANSEY (1)

Thomas Dawson's *The good Huswifes Handmaide for the Kitchin*, 1594

'To make a Tansey. Take a little tansy*, feverfew, parsley and violets, and stamp them all together. Strain them with the yolks of 8 or 10 eggs, and 3 or 4 whites, & some verjuice, and put thereto sugar and salt, and fry it.'

*Tansy (*Tanacetum vulgare*) is a perennial herbaceous flowering plant of the aster family, also known as common tansy, bitter buttons, cow bitter or golden buttons. At Easter, even archbishops and bishops played handball with men of their congregation, and a tansy cake was the reward of the victors. These cakes were made from the young leaves of the plant, mixed with eggs, and were thought to purify the humours of the body after the limited fare of Lent. Tansies, as these cakes were called, came to be eaten on Easter Day as a remembrance of the bitter herbs eaten by the Jews at the Passover. Coles in 1656 wrote that the origin of eating it in the spring is because tansy was very wholesome after the salt fish consumed during Lent, and counteracted the ill effects which the 'moist and cold constitution of winter has made on people ... though many understand it not, and some simple people take it for a matter of superstition to do so'.

A TANSEY (2)

Thomas Dawson's *The good Huswifes Handmaide for the Kitchin*, 1594

'To make a Tansey another way. Take half a handful of tansy, of the youngest ye can get, and a handful of young borage, strawberry leaves, lettuce, and violet leaves. Wash them clean, and beat them very small in a mortar. Then put to them 8 eggs, whites and all, and 6 yolks besides, and strain them all together through a strainer. Then season it with a good handful of sugar, and a nutmeg beaten small. Then take a frying pan, and half a dish of sweet butter, and melt it. Then put your eggs to it, set it on the fire, and with a saucer, or with a ladle, stir them till they be half baked. Then put them into a platter, and all to beat them still till they be very small. Then take your frying pan made clean, and put a dish of sweet butter in it, and melt it. Then put your stuff into your pan by a spoonful at once, and when the one side is fried, turn them and fry them together. Then take them out, lay them in a platter, and scrape sugar on them.

COMFITMAKERS' BISKET

A Closet for Ladies and Gentlewomen, 1602

'To make the usuall bisket solde at Comfitmakers*. Take a peck of flour and 4 ounces of coriander seed, 1 ounce of aniseed, take 3 egges, 3 spoonfuls of ale yeast, and as much warm water as will make it as thick as pastry for manchets. Make it in a long roll, and bake it in an oven for one hour. When it is a day old pare it, and slice it. Sugar it with sieved sugar, and put it again into the oven, and when it is dry, take it out, and new sugar it again, and so box it and keep it.'

*Comfitmakers provided the sweets and biscuits for banquets.

FINE BREAD

Thomas Dawson's *The Good Huswifes Jewell*, 1596

'To make fine bread. Take half a pound of fine sugar well beaten, and as much flour, and put thereto 4 egg whites, being very well beaten. You must mingle them with bruised aniseeds, and being all beaten together, put into your mould, melting the sauce over first with a little butter, and set it in the oven. Turn it twice or thrice in the baking.'

FINE MANCHET

Thomas Dawson's *The good Huswifes Handmaide for the Kitchin*, 1594

'The making of fine Manchet. Take half a bushel of fine flour twice bolted, and a gallon of fair lukewarm water,

Opposite: 21. Confectioners at work in York, probably in the Archbishop's Palace kitchens, depicted here in 1595.

God blesseth trewe labour,
With plentye and fauour.

Be still quicke and kinde
Reward thou shalt finde

Pricke not at thy pleasure,
But in trewe honest meature

Be watchfull and wise
In goodnelle to zise:

In heauen shall haue a place to dwell:

almost a handful of white salt, and almost a pint of yeast. Then temper all these together, without any more liquor, as hard as ye can handle it. Then let it lie half an hour, then take it up, and make your manchets, and let them stande almost an hour in the oven. Memorandum, that from every bushel of meal may be made 25 casts of bread, and every loaf to weigh a pound.'

[Manchet was the bread of the nobility, the finest-quality white bread, often formed into flattish round loaves. It is also recorded being spelt as: manged, maunchett, maynche, maynchett, mayned, mengyd, meyned, manchete, manchett, mainchet, mancheat, mancheate, manched, manchuet, mayngate, maunchet, maincheat, manchent, manshut, manchette, manchit, mainchott, mainschoitt, mainschot, mainschott, manschet, manschot, manshote, manshott, mayneshet, mayneshott, maynshott, meaneschot, meaneschott, menschatt and menschoitt.]

THE MAKING OF MANCHETS AFTER MY LADIE GRAIES USE

Thomas Dawson's *The good Huswifes Handmaide for the Kitchin*, 1594

'The making of manchets after my Ladie Graies use. Take two pecks of fine flour, which must be twice bolted, if you will have your manchet very fair. Then lay it in a place where ye do use to lay your dough for your bread, and make a little hole in it, and put in that water as much leaven as a crab, or a pretty big apple, and as much white salt as will into an eggshell, and all to break your leaven in the water. And put into your flour half a pint of good ale yeast. And so stir this liquor among a little of your flour, so that ye must make it but thin at the first meeting, and then cover it with flour. And if it be in the winter, ye must keep it very warm, and in summer it shall not need so much heat, for in the winter it will not rise without warmth. Thus let it lie two hours and a half. Then at the second opening take more liquor as ye think will serve to wet all the flour. Then put in a pint and a half of good yeast, and so all to break it in short pieces, after ye have well laboured it, and wrought it 5 or 6 times, so that ye be sure it is throughly mingled together. So continue labouring it, till it come to a smooth paste, and be well aware at the second opening that ye put not in too much liquor suddenly, for then it wil run, and if ye take a little it will be stiff. And after the second working it must lie a good quarter of an hour, and keep it warm. Then take it up to the moulding board, and with as much speed as is possible to be made, mould it up, and set it into the oven. Of one peck of flour ye may make 10 casts of manchets fair and good.'

LEAVENED BREAD

Thomas Dawson's *The good Huswifes Handmaide for the Kitchin*, 1594

'To make leavened bread. Take 6 yolks of eggs, and a little piece of butter as big as a walnut, one handful of very fine flour, and make all these in pastry, and all to beat it with a rolling pin, till it be as thin as a paper leaf. Then take sweet butter and melt it, and rub over all your pastry therewith, with a feather. Then roll up your pastry softly as ye would roll up a scroll of paper. Then cut them in pieces of three inches long, and make them flat with your hands and lay them upon a sheet of clean paper. Bake them in an oven or pan, but the oven may

He that giueth meafure,
God bleſſeth with treafure.

It makes a poore man,
To ſell flower for bran.

Looke well to thy ſeaſon,
with cunninge and reaſon.

Be iuſt with thy weightes,
God plagues falſe ſleightes.

not be too hot, and they must bake half an hour. Then take some sweet butter and melt it, and put that into your pastry when it comes out of the oven, and when they are very wet, so that they be not dry, take them out of your butter, and lay them in a fair dish, and cast upon them a little sugar, and if you please, cinnamon and ginger, and serve them forth.'

PIE PASTRY

A Proper New Booke of Cookery, 1545 and 1575

'To make short paste for a Tart. Take fine flour, a litle fair water, & a dish of sweet butter, & a little saffron, and the yolks of two eggs, & make it thin and as tender as ye may.'

FINE PASTRY COFFINS

Thomas Dawson's *The Second part of The Good Huswifes Jewell*, 1597

'To make fine paste. Take fair flour and wheat, & the yolks of eggs with sweet butter, melted, mixing all these together with your hands, till it be brought to dough pastry. Then make your coffins whether it be for pies or tarts. Then you may put saffron and sugar if you will have a sweet paste, having respect to the true seasoning. Some use to put to their pastry beef or mutton broth, and some cream.'

Opposite: 22. Bakers at York sieving grain, and stretching, working and weighing dough. Only men worked in the kitchens of gentry, clergy and nobility. This illustration dates from 1595–6.

TO MAKE PASTE, AND RAISE COFFINS

Thomas Dawson's *The good Huswifes Handmaide for the Kitchin*, 1594

'To make Paste, and to raise Coffins. Take fine flour, and lay it on a board. Take a certain amount of yolks of eggs as your quantity of flower is, then take a certain amount of butter and water, and boil them together. But ye must take heed ye put not too many yolks of eggs, for if you do, it will make it dry and not pleasant in eating. And ye must take heed ye put not in too much butter for if you do, it will make it so fine and so short that it cannot raise. And this pastry is good to raise all manner of coffins. Likewise if ye bake venison, bake it in the pastry above named.'

FINE PASTE ANOTHER WAY

Thomas Dawson's *The good Huswifes Handmaide for the Kitchin*, 1594

'To make fine Paste a nother way. Take butter and ale, and seethe them together. Then take your flour, and add three eggs, sugar, saffron and salt.'

SHORT PASTE IN LENT

Thomas Dawson's *The good Huswifes Handmaide for the Kitchin*, 1594

'To make short paste in Lent. Take thick almond milk seething hot, and so wet your flour with it, and salad oil fried, and saffron, and so mingle your pastry altogether, and that will make good pastry.'

FINE CRACKNELS

Thomas Dawson's *The Good Huswifes Jewell*, 1596

'To make fine cracknels. Take fine flour and a good quantity of eggs, as many as will supply the flour. Then take as much sugar as will sweeten the pastry, and if you will not be at the cost to raise it with eggs, and put thereto sweet water, cinnamon and a good quantity of nutmeges and mace, according to your bread. Take a good quantity of aniseeds, and let all this be blended with your flour, and the adding in of your eggs or other moisture. Then set on your water and let it be at seething, before you add your crackneles in it. They will sink to the bottom. And at their rising, take them out and dry them with a cloth, then bake them.'

APOLLO.

ÆSCVLAPIV

A NIEVVE HERBALL,
OR HISTORIE OF PLANTES:

wherin is contayned

the vvhole discourse and perfect description of all sortes of Herbes
and Plantes; their diuers & sundry kindes:
their straunge Figures, Fashions, and Shapes:
their Names / Natures / Operations / and Vertues: and that not onely of those whiche are
here growing in this our Countrie of
Englande / but of all others also of
forrayne Realmes / commonly
vsed in Physicke.

First set foorth in the Doutche or Almaigne
tongue, by that learned D. Rembert Do-
doens, Physition to the Emperour:
And nowe first translated out of
French into English, by Henry Lyte Esquyer.

AT LONDON

by me Gerard Dewes, dwelling in
Pawles Churchyarde at the signe
of the Swanne.

1578

METRI-
DATES

LYSIMACH

HESPERIDVM HORTI

10

Butters, Sauces, Pickles, Conserves and Preserves

ALMOND BUTTER

Thomas Dawson's *The Good Huswifes Jewell*, 1596

'To make Almond butter. Take almonds and blanch them, and beat them in a mortar very small, and in the beating put in a little water. And when they be beaten, pour in water into two pots, and put in half into one and half into another, and put in sugar, and stir them still. And let them boil a good while, then strain it through a strainer with rose water, and so dish it up.'

ALMOND BUTTER AFTER THE BEST AND NEWEST FASHION

Thomas Dawson's *The good Huswifes Handmaide for the Kitchin*, 1594

'To make Almond butter after the best and newest manner. Take a pound of almonds or more, as ye will. Blanch them in cold water, or in warm, as ye may have

Opposite: 23. The title page of Lyte's translation of Dodoen's Herbal, published in English in 1578. Herbals came to prominence in the Tudor period, widening understanding of the properties of different herbs.

leisure. After the blanching, let them lie an hour in cold water. Then stamp them in fair cold water as fine as ye can. Then put your almonds in a cloth, and gather your cloth round up in your hands, and press out the milk, as much as you can. If ye think they be not small enough, beat them again, and so get out milk as long as you can. Then set it on the fire, and when it is ready to seethe, put in a good quantity of salt, and rosewater, that will turn it. And after it is in, let it have one boiling, and then take it from the fire, and cast it abroad upon a linen cloth, and underneath the cloth, scrape off the whey as long as it will run. Then scrape together the butter into the midst of your cloth, and bind the cloth together, and let it hang as long as it will drop. Then take pieces of sugar, as much as ye think will make it sweet, and add thereto rosewater a little, as much as will melt the sugar, and fine powder of saffron, as ye think will colour it. And let both your sugar and saffron steep together in that little quantity of rosewater, & with that season up your butter when you will make it.'

WHITE AND YELLOW EGG BUTTER
Thomas Dawson's *The Second part of The Good Huswifes Jewell*, 1597
'To make buttered Eggs. Take 8 yolks of eggs, and put them into a pint of cream, beat them together and strain them into a posnet all, setting upon the fire and stirring. Let it seethe until it quails, then take it and put it into a clean cloth, and let it hang so that the whey may avoid from it. And when it is gone beat it into a dish of rosewater and sugar, with a spoon, and so shall you have fine butter. This done, you may take the white of the same eggs, adding it into another pint of cream, using it as the yolks were used,

and thus you may have as fine white butter as you have yellow butter.'

PIGGESAUCE – SPICED APPLE SAUCE FOR PORK
The Good Hous-wiues Treasurie, 1588
'Piggesauce. Take half vineger, and half verjuice, a handful of parsely, sage chopped very small, and a pomewater [an extinct type of apple]. Shred very small, then take the gravy of the pig, with sugar and pepper and boil them together.'

PORK SAUCE
The Good Hous-wiues Treasurie, 1588
'Porke Sauce. Take vinegar, mustard, sugar and pepper.'

PUR VERDE SAWCE – GREEN SAUCE
A Noble Boke off Cookry ffor a Prynce Houssolde Holkham, MSS 674, 1480/1500
'To mak vert sauce. Take parsley, mint, sorell, chives and sauce alone. Then take bred and steep it in vinegar. Add thereto pepper and salt, and grind them and temper them up and serve it.'
[Now unfashionable, green was a very popular colour in medieval cooking, and this author has had some superb green sauce dishes at Adolf Wagner's *apfelwein* (scrumpy cider) restaurant in Sachsenhausen, Frankfurt. This sauce was the preferred shade of green, tinted with yellow, sometimes called *vertgay*. If the flavour is a little sharp, replace some or all of the vinegar with more white wine. Basically almost any herbs were used, according to season. Green sauce appears in recipes across Europe from the

twelfth century, and was often favoured with fish dishes. Please try it!]

SAUCE FOR A GOOCE
The Good Hous-wiues Treasurie, 1588
'Sauce for a Gooce. Take vinegar and apples shred very small, two spoonfuls of mustard, a little pepper and salt. Take sugar sufficient to sweeten it, then boil it well together.'

CAPON SAUCE
The Good Hous-wiues Treasurie, 1588
'Capon sauce. Take water, onions, pepper, and some of the gravy and salt, and boil them together.'

SYRUPE OF LYMONDS
A Closet for Ladies and Gentlewomen, 1602
'To make Syrupe of Lymonds. Take your lemons*, and cut them in half, and betwixt your fingers juice them, and the liquor that runs from them wil be very clear. Then take to a pint of juice, a pound and a quarter of hard sugar, which is very white and boil it to a syrup, and it will keep excellent well.'
*Lymond may equally apply to limes at this time, and either can be used.

PEAR CONSERVE
Thomas Dawson's *The Second part of The Good Huswifes Jewell*, 1597
'To conserve wardens all the yeere in sirrop. Take your wardens [hard pears] and put them into a great

earthenware pot, and cover them close. Set them in an oven when you have set in your white bread. And when you have drawn your white bread, and your pot, & they are so cold that you may handle them, then peel the thin skin from them over a pewter dish, so you may save all the syrup that falls from them. Add to them a quart of the same syrup, and a pint of rosewater, and boil them together with a few cloves and cinnamon. When it is reasonably thick and cold, put your wardens and syrup into a galley pot [a small glazed earthenware jar], and see always that the syrup is above the wardens, or any other thing that you conserve.'

CHERRY, DAMSON OR PLUM CONSERVE

Thomas Dawson's *The Second part of The Good Huswifes Jewell*, 1597

'To conserve cherries, Damesins or wheat plummes* all the yeere in the sirrop. First take fair water, so much as you shall think meet, and one pound of sugar, and put them both into a fair bason. And set the same over a soft fire, till the sugar be melted. Then put thereto one pound and a half of cherries, or damsons, and let them boil till they break. Then cover them close till they be cold, then put them in your galley pots, and so keep them. In this way keeping proportion in weight of sugar and fruit, you may conserve as much as you wish putting thereto cinnamon and cloves, as is aforesaid.'

*The wheat plum is listed among plum varieties in the 1728 *Dictionarium Botanicum*, but appears to be extinct. Under 'w' in a recent book, the only listings are Willingham gage, Wallis's Wonder plum and the Warwickshire Drooper plum.

TO PRESERVE RED APPLES
A Closet for Ladies and Gentlewomen, 1602

'To preserve Pippyns red. Take your best coloured pippins and pare them, then take a piercer and bore a hole through them. Then make syrup for them, as much as will cover them, and so let them boile in a broad preserving pan. Put into them a piece of cinnamon stick, and so let them boil close covered very leisurely, turning them very often. For if you turn them not very often, they will pot, and the one side will not be like the other. And let them thus boil, until they begin to jelly, then take them up, and pot them, and you may keep them all the year.'

TO PRESERVE APRICOCKES AND PEAR-PLUMS
A Closet for Ladies and Gentlewomen, 1602

'To preserve Apricockes. Take a pound of apricots, and a pound of sugar, and clarify your sugar with a pint of water. When your sugar is made perfect, put it into a preserving-pan, & put your apricots into it and so let them boil gently. And when they be boyled enough and your syrup thick, pot them and so keep them. In like manner may you preserve a pear-plum.'

DRIE MARMELET OF PECHES
Thomas Dawson's *The Second part of The Good Huswifes Jewell*, 1597

'To make drie Marmelet of Peches. Take your peaches and pare them, and cut them from the stones, and mince them very finely, and steep them in rosewater. Then strain them with rosewater through a coarse cloth or strainer into your pan that you will seethe it in. You must have, to every pound of peaches, half a pound of sugar

24. Cherries, an apricot and a lemon pictured in a sixteenth-century engraving by Jacob Hoefnagel.

finely beaten. Put it into your pan that you boil it in. You must reserve out a good quantity to mould your cakes or prints withall, of that sugar. Then set your pan on the fire, and stir it till it be so thick or stiff that your stick will stand upright in it of itself. Then take it up and lay it in a platter or charger in pretty lumps, as big as you will have ye mould or prints. When it is cold print it on a fair board with sugar, and print them on a mould or what knot or fashion you will. And bake in an earthenware pot or pan upon ye embers or in a seat cover, and keep them continually by the fire to keep them dry.'

DRIE MARMELET OF QUINCES
Thomas Dawson's *The Second part of The Good Huswifes Jewell*, 1597
'To make the same of Quinces, or any other thing. Take the quinces and quarter them, and cut out the cores and pare them clean, and seethe them in fair water till they be

very tender. Then take them with rosewater, and strain them, and do as is aforesaid in everything.'

TO PRESERVE CHERRIES
A Closet for Ladies and Gentlewomen, 1602

'To preserve Cherries. Take of the best and fairest cherries some two pounds, and with a pair of shears clip off the stalks by the midst, then wash them clean, and beware you bruise them not. Then take fine barbary sugar, and set it over the fire with a quart of fair water in the broadest vessel you can get, and let it seethe till it be somewhat thick. Then put in your cherries, and stir them together with a silver spoon and so let them boil, always skimming, and turning them very gently, that the one side may be like the other, until they be ready. To know when, you must take up some of the syrup with one cherry, and so let it cool, and if it will scarce run out it is ready. And thus being cold, you may put them up, and keep them all the year.'

TO PRESERVE RASPISES
A Closet for Ladies and Gentlewomen, 1602

'To preserve Raspises. Take your fairest and well coloured raspberries, and pick off their stalks very clean, then wash them, but in any case see that you bruise them not. Then weigh them, and to every pound of raspberries you must take 6 ounces of hard sugar, and 6 ounces of sugar-candy, & clarify it with half a pint of fair water, and 4 ounces of juice of raspberries. Being clarified, boil it to a weak syrup, and then put in your raspberries, stirring them up and down, and so let them boil until they be ready. That is, using them as your cherries, and so may you keep them all the year.'

CHERRY OR BARBERRY CONSERVE

John Partridge's *The Treasurie of commodious Conceits*, 1573

'To make conserve of Cheries and Barberries. Likewise ye must make conserve of cherries, and also of barberries saving that these require more sugar than the other does, which are not so sour as they be. Here is to be noted, that of conserves of fruits may be made marmalade, for when your conserve is sufficiently sodden, and ready to be taken off, then seeth it more on height and it will be marmalade. Moreover some make their conserve, marmalade & syrups with clean sugar, some with clean honey clarified, some with sugar and honey together. And after the opinion of divers great clerks, honey is more wholesome, though it be not so toothsome as sugar.'

PRESERVE OF ORRENGES, WALNUTS, LEMONS AND POMESITRONS

Thomas Dawson's *The Second part of The Good Huswifes Jewell*, 1597

'To preserve Orrenges, Lemons, and Pomesitrons. First shave your oranges finely, & put them into water 2 days and 2 nights, changing your water 3 times a day. Then parboil them in 3 several waters, then take so much water as you think convenient for the quantity of your oranges. Then put in for every pound of oranges one pound and a half of sugar into the water. Put in two whites of eggs and beat them all together, then set them on the fire in a brass vessel. When they boil skim them very clean, and cleanse them through a jelly bag. Then set it on the fire and put in the oranges. Use walnuts in like manner, and use lemons and pomecitrons* in like sort, but they must lie in water just one night.'

*The pomecitron/pomme citron was a variety of cooking apple.

TO PRESERVE ORANGES AND LYMONDS
A Closet for Ladies and Gentlewomen, 1602
'To preserve Oranges and Lymonds. Take your oranges and lemons large and well coloured, and take a rasp of steel, and rasp the outward rind from them. Then lay them in water 3 days and 3 nights. Then boil them tender and shift them in the boiling to take away their bitterness. And when they be boiled tenderly, take 2 pound of sugar clarified with a pint of water, and when your syrup is made, and betwixt hot and cold, put in your lemons and oranges. And there let them be infused all night, the next morning let them boil two or three walmes [a walme is a period of boiling/bubbling] in your syrup. Let them not boil too long in the sugar, because the rinds will be tough. Take your lemons out and boyle your syrupe thicker. And so when it is cold, put them up and keep them all the year.'

TO PRESERVE PEACHES
A Closet for Ladies and Gentlewomen, 1602
'To preserve Peaches. Take a pound of your fairest and best coloured peaches, and with a wet linen cloth wipe off the white hoar [fuzz] from them, then parboil them in half a pint of white wine, and a pint and a half of running water. Being parboiled, peel off the white skin, and then weigh them. Take to your pound of peaches, ¾ of a pound of refined sugar, and dissolve it in a ¼ of a pint of white

wine, and boil it almost to the height of a syrup. Then put in your peaches, and let them boil in the syruop a quarter of an hour or more if need should require, and then put them up, and keepe them all the year.'

TO PRESERVE GOOS-BERRIES

A Closet for Ladies and Gentlewomen, 1602

'To preserve Goos-berries. Take your large berries, but not thoroughly ripe, and pick off all the stalks from them. Wash them clean, take a pound of them, and set them on the fire, till they be hot. Then take them off, and let the liquor run from them. Then take 10 ounces of hard sugar, and 4 ounces of sugar Candy, and clarify it with a pint of water and the white of an egg, and boil it to a thick syrup. Then put in your gooseberries, and let them bole for a period or two, and so betwixt hot and cold, put them up, & keep them all the year.'

DAMSON AND OTHER MARMALADES

John Partridge's *The Treasurie of commodious Conceits*, 1573

'To make Marmalade of Damasines or Prunes. Take damsons which are ripe. Boil them on the fire with a little fair water till they be soft, then draw them through a coarse bolter. As ye make a tart set it on the fire again. Seethe it on height with sufficient sugar, as you do your quinces, dash it with sweet water & co. and box it. If you will make it of prunes, even likewise do put some apples also to it, as you did to your quinces. This way you may make marmalade of wardens, pears, apples & medlars, servits* or checkers**, strawberries every one by himself, or else mixed together, as you think good.'

*Sorbus domestica is the service tree, or sometimes 'true service tree' to distinguish it from the wild service tree, and is almost extinct in Britain. The fruit is a component of a cider-like drink is still made in parts of Europe. Picked straight off the tree, it is highly astringent and gritty; however, when left to 'blet' (overripen like medlars) it sweetens and becomes pleasant to eat. While Partridge calls the fruits servuits or servits, other English names for the tree include sorb, sorb tree, and whitty pear, 'pear' due to the appearance of the small fruit.

**Sorbus torminalis, sometimes known as the chequer tree or checker tree had edible fruit, sometimes called chequers, which are edible and taste similar to dates, although they are now rarely collected for food and the tree is rare. They usually need bletting. Before the introduction of hops, the fruit were used to flavour beer, which may be related to the ancient symbol of a pub being the chequer board. Alternatively, the name 'chequers' may have been derived from the spotted pattern of the fruit, though some suggest it comes from the pattern of the bark on old trees.

[The word marmalade comes from *marmelo*, the Portuguese for quince, and the first marmalade was a quince preserve.]

TO PRESERVE DAMSINS
A Closet for Ladies and Gentlewomen, 1602

'To preserve Damsins. Take your damsons large and well coloured, but not thoroughly ripe, for then they will break, and pick them clean and wipe them one by one. Then weigh them, and to every pound of damsons, you must take a pound of Barbary sugar white & good, & dissolved in half a pint or more of water, and boil it almost to the height of a syrup. Then put in your damsons, keeping them with continual skimming, and stirring, and that with a silver spoon. And so let them boil until they be ready upon a gentle fire, take them up, & keep them all the year.

STRAWBERRY CONSERVE

John Partridge's *The Treasurie of commodious Conceits*, 1573

'To make conserve of Strawberies, With the vertue of the same. Take strawberries, 1 quart clean picked and washed. Set them on the fire till they be soft, strain them put thereto two times as much sugar in powder, as weight of the strawberries. Let them seethe till the sugar be incorporated with the strawberries. Put it in a glass or earthenware pot well glazed. The virtue of the same. The conserve of strawberries is good against a hot liver, or burning of the stomach, and especially in the fervent heat of an ague.'

QUEEN MARY TUDOR'S MARMALADE

A Closet for Ladies and Gentlewomen, 1602

'To make an excellent Marmelate which was given Queene Mary for a New-yeares gift. Take a pound and half of sugar, boil it with a pint of fair water till it comes to the height of Manus Christi. Then take 3 or 4 small quinces, one good orange peel, both very well preserved and finely beaten, & 3 ounces of almonds blanched and beaten by themselues, eryngo roots* preserved, two ounces and a half. Stir these with the sugar till it will not stick, and then at the last put in musk and amber[gris], dissolved in rosewater, of each 4 grains.

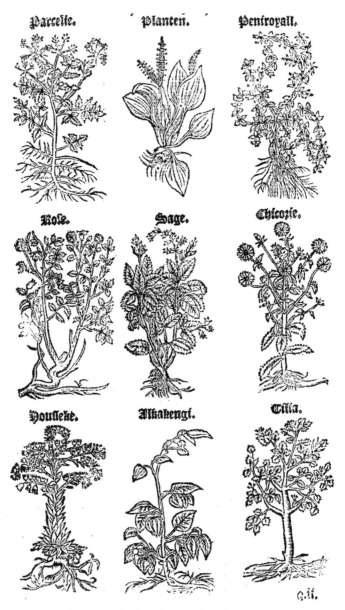

25. A sixteenth-century herb index. Herbs of all sorts were used both in medical concoctions and in food and drink, with reference to their use in the 'Doctrine of Humours'.

Add of cinnamon, ginger, cloves and mace, of each 3 drammes, and of oil of cynnamon 2 drops. This being done, put it into your marmelade boxes, and so present it to whom you please.

*Eryngo is sea holly, *Eryngium maritimum*, used for many ailments in medieval times – see *The Physicians of Myddfai* (2013) by this author for the use of herbs in illness at this time.

[Marmalade of this sort was thought to be an aphrodisiac, and the queen could not conceive.]

VIOLET CONSERVE
A Closet for Ladies and Gentlewomen, 1602

'To make Conserve of Violets. Take your violet flowers, and pick off all the blue flowers, and keep them and weigh them. And take to every ounce of flowers 3 ounces of refined sugar, and beat them in an alabaster mortar till they be very fine, and then take them up and put them into an earthenware pipkin, and set them upon the fire untill such time as they be thoroughy hoe. Then take them off, and put them up and keep them.'

ROSEMARY FLOWER CONSERVE
A Closet for Ladies and Gentlewomen, 1602

'To make conserve of Rosemary flowers. Take your rosemary flowers, fresh and good and pick them from the greene tusk. Weigh them, and take to every ounce of flowers 3 ounces of sugar-candy, and beat them very fine, using them in every respect as you did your other conserves.'

SEROP OF ROSES – ROSE JAM
Elinor Fettiplace's *Receipt Book*, 1604

'To Make A Serop Of Roses. Take damask rose buds 6 handfuls, & cut off the tops, and take a quart of fair running water, & put the roses therein. Put them in a basin & set them over the fire, that the water may be warm one day and night. Then in the morning squeeze the roses hard between your hands out of the water, & put in as many fresh, & let them stand still on the fire. This do 9 times, then take out your roses, clean out of the water, & put in as much sugar as will make it sweet. Boil it till it comes to a syrup; you must put to every pint a pound of sugar.'

BARBERRY CONSERVE
A Closet for Ladies and Gentlewomen, 1602

'To make Conserve of Barberies. Take your barberries which are very red and ripe and pick them from the stalks and then wash them and put unto them a pretty deal of fair water. Set them on the fire in an earthenware pan and so scald them. Being throughly scalded, pulp them thorough a fine sieve, and to every pound of pulp take a pound of powdered sugar and boil till it be ready, that is, till it wil cut like marmelade.'

GALLENTYNE SAUCE – MULTIPURPOSE TUDOR SAUCE
Gentyll Manly Cokere, MS Pepys 1047, *c.* 1490

'To make gallentyne. Take crusts of white sour bread and toast it till hit be brown and steep it in vinegar. Draw through a strainer with the same vinegar. Set on the fire and boil well and cast therein sanders, powder of ginger, cinnamon and a little pepper. And if it be too tart add more sugar and that will amend it.'

VINEGAR OF ROSES AND OTHER FLOWERS

John Partridge's *The Treasurie of commodious Conceits*, 1573
'To make Vineger of Roses. In Summer time when roses
blow, gather them ere they be full spread or blown out,
and in dry weather. Pluck the leaves, let them lie half a
day upon a fayre borde [table]. Then have a vessel with
vinegar of one or two gallons (if you will make so much
roset). Put therein a great quantity of the said leaves,
snd stop the vessel close after you have stirred them well
together. Let it stand a day and a night. Then divide your
vinegar & rose leaves together in two parts. Put them in
two great glasses & put in rose leaves [petals] enough.
Stop the glasses close, set them upon a shelf under a wall
side, on the Southside without your house where the Sun
may come to them the most part of the day. Let them
stand there all the whole summer long. Then strain the
vinegar from the roses, and keep the vinegar. If you shall,
once in 10 days, take and strain out the rose leaves, and
put in newe leaves of half a day's gathering, the vinegar
will have the more flavour and odour of the rose. You
may use instead of vinegar, wine, that it may wax eager,
and receive ye virtue of the roses, both at once. Moreover,
you may make your vinegar of wine white, red, or claret,
but the red doth most bind the belly, & white doth most
loosen. Also the Damaske rose is not so great a binder
as the red rose, and the white rose the most loose of all,
whereof you may make roset [rosé] vinegar. Thus also,
you may make vinegar of violets, or of elder flowers: but
you must first gather & use your flowers of elder, as shall
be showed hereafter, when we speak of making conserve
of elder flowers.'

WHITE OR RED VINEGER
The Good Hous-wiues Treasurie, 1588

'How to make white or red Vineger. Fetch your vinegar at Saint Katherines a groat a gallon to the quantity of 6 gallons. Add thereto a pottle of elder flowers such as will shake off when they be ripe, and see your vessel be close stopped up and filled. And thus you maye renew your vessel every year with vinegar and flowers according to the quantity but let the old remain. This maye you do either with strong or small beer and the remnants of barrels.'

PICKLED COWCUMBERS
A Closet for Ladies and Gentlewomen, 1602

'To keepe Cowcumbers in pickle all the yeare. Take 4 gallons of conduit water and put unto it 3 quarts of bay salt, 2 handfuls of sage, one handful of sweet marjoram, and 4 handfuls of dill. Let these boil till it come to 3 gallons, and then take it off. And when it is almost cold, put in 100 cucumbers into that liquor, into a butter barrel & keep them all the year, but look that always the herbs lie upon them. And thus done, it will be a most excellent salad with oil, vinegar and pepper.'

11

Miscellaneous

These are obviously not food recipes, but are irresistible.

BUTTERED BEERE
Thomas Dawson's *The good Huswifes Handmaide for the Kitchin*, 1594
'To make Buttered Beere. Take 3 pints of Beere, add 5 yolks of Eggs to it, strain them together, and set it in a pewter pot to the fire. And put to it half a pound of sugar, one pennyworth of nutmegs beaten, one penniworth of cloves beaten, and a halfpennyworth of ginger beaten. And when it is all in, take another pewter pot and brew them together, and set it to the fire again, and when it is ready to boil, take it from the fire, and put a dish of sweet butter into it, and brew them together out of one pot into another.'
[This was a drink for invalids, or a breakfast drink. For those confused with halfpennies, this author remembers farthings as legal currency – there were 960 to the pound and the obverse of the king's head was a robin ...]

... AND ONE FOR THE HEALTH-CONSCIOUS – A SLIMMING SMOOTHIE FOR ALL OF US

Thomas Dawson's *The Good Huswifes Jewell*, 1596

'For to make one slender. Take fennel, and seethe it in water, a very good quantity, and wring out the juice thereof when it is boiled. Drink it first and last [morning and night] and it shall swage* either him or her.'

*You shape metal, especially reducing a cross-section, by using a tool called a *swage*.

... AND ONE FOR THE HORTICULTURALIST – POMPONS, MELON- OR CUCUMBER-SEED SWEETS

Thomas Dawson's *The Second part of The Good Huswifes Jewell*, 1597

'To make Mellons and Pompons sweet. Take fine sugar and dissolve it in water, then take seeds of melons and cleave them a little on the side that sticks to the melon. And put them in the sugared water, adding to them a little rosewater. Leave the said seeds so by the space of 3 or 4 hours, then take them out, and you shall see that as soon as the said seeds be dry, it wil close up again. Plant it and there will come of it such melons, as the like hath not been seen. If you will have them to give the savour of musk, put in the said water a little musk, and fine cinnamon, and thus you may do the seeds of pompones [chrysanthemum] and cucumbers.'

... AND SOME TUDOR REMEDIES FOR THE FOLLICALLY CHALLENGED

As someone who has white thinning hair and a bald patch, I have shared the angst of many men, and thus noticed the many remedies for hair loss given by the Physicians of

Myddfai. Indeed, a successful anti-hair-loss product would make the patentee a multi-billionaire almost overnight. Among the virtues of mustard the physicians note that 'it is good for colic, loss of hair, noise in the ears, and dimness of sight, cutaneous eruptions, palsy, and many other things'. Other remedies include:

FOR ALOPECIA

'Take watercress*, bruise well and express the juice. Wash your head therewith and scrub it well. The same juice may also be taken internally, and you will be cured.'

*Watercress is a traditional cure for hair loss, owing to the presence of biotin (vitamin B7) and zinc, and therefore is present in many modern shampoos. It also contains iron, silica and pyridoxine (vitamin B6). The deficiency of any or all of these components can cause alopecia.

TO CAUSE THE HAIR TO GROW

'Take barberry (*Berberis vulgaris*) and fill an iron pot with it. Fill it up with as much water as it will contain, then boil on a slow fire until reduced to half. With this water, wash your head morning and evening. Take care that the wash does not touch any part where hair should not grow.'

TO CAUSE THE HAIR TO GROW (2)

'Take two spoonfuls of olive oil, two spoonfuls of new honey, and an onion as large as a pigeon's egg. Pound them together in a stone mortar till it becomes an ointment, and anoint your head therewith night and morning. Wear a leather cap until the hair is grown. It is best to pound the onion well before it is added to the ointment.'

TO CAUSE THE HAIR TO GROW (3)

'Shave the head clean with a razor, and take honey with the juice of onions in equal parts. Anoint and scrub the head well with the same every morning and night. The head should be washed with the distilled water of honey. It is proven.'

TO CAUSE THE HAIR TO GROW (4)

'Shave the head carefully, anoint with honey, and sprinkle the powder of mollipuffs* upon it.'

*Mollipuffs were called by Pughe *Lycoperdon Bovista*, now known as the Warted Puffball fungus, *Bovista officinalis*.

Sources

[N.B. If you type into Google a part of any title of the primary sources, you will usually reach a digitised text, or one of the many medieval cookery sites related to the texts.]

PRIMARY SOURCES

c. 1490: *Gentyll Manly Cokere* AND COPYD OF THE SERGENT TO THE KYNG [MS Pepys 1047]

1500: *THIS IS THE BOKE OF COKERY.* Here beginneth a noble boke of festes royalle and Cokery a boke for a pryncis housholde or any other estates; and the makynge therof as ye shall fjmde more playnly within this boke. Emprynted without temple barre by Richard Pynson in the yere of our lorde. MD. [The same book, printed between 1533 and 1540, was printed by John Byddell and called *A noble booke of feastes royall, and of Cookerie, for Princes housholde, or any other estate, and the making thereof.*]

1508: *HERE BEGYNNETH THE BOKE OF KERVYNGE.* [The colophon is 'Here endeth the boke of servyce and kervynge and sewynge and all maner of offyce in his kynde unto a prynce or ony other estate and all the feestes in the yere. Emprynted by Wynkyn de Worde at London in the Fletestrete at the sygne of the sonne. The yere of our lorde, M.CCCC.VIII'. The book was added in 1597 to *The second part of the Good Hus-wifes Jewell*, and in 1631 to John Murrell's *Two bookes of cookerie and carving*.]

1545: *A PROPER NEWE BOOKE OF COKERYE*, declarynge what maner of meates be beste in season, for al times in the yere, and how they ought to be dressed, and serued at the table, bothe for fleshe dayes, and fyshe dayes. With a newe addition, verye necessarye for all them that delyghteth in Cokerye. [The first owner of the book was Matthew Parker, Archbishop of Canterbury, and it was used by his wife Margaret Parker.]

1558: *THE SECRETES OF THE REVERENDE MAISTER ALEXIS OF PIEMONT*. Containyng excellente remedies against divers diseases, woundes, and other accidents, with the manner to make distilations, parfumes, confitures, diynges, colours, fusions and raeltynges. A worke well approved, verye profytable and necessary for every man. Translated out of French into English, by Willyam Warde. Imprynted at London by John Kingstone for Nicolas Inglande, dwellinge in Poules Churchyarde. Anno 1558. Menss. Novemb.

1562: *Here foloweth A COMPEDYOUS REGYMENT OR A DYETARY OF HELTH*, made in Mofitpylior: compiled by Andrewe Boorde, of Physicke Doctor. [The earliest edition has no date, and the next is dated 1562.]

1573, 1580, 1584, 1586, 1591, 1594, 1596: *THE TREASURIE OF COMMODIOUS CONCEITES, AND HIDDEN SECRETS*. Commonly called The Good Huswives Closet of provision for the health of her houshold. Meete and necessarie for the profitable use of all estates, gathered out of sundry Experiments lately practised by men of great knowledge ... These Bookes are to be sould at the West ende of Paules Church: By Richard

Jones, the Printer hereof, 1573. By John Partridge. [The book later appears as *THE TREASURIE OF HIDDEN SECRETS. Commonlie called, The good-huswives Closet of provision, for the health of her Houshold.* Gathered out of sundry experiments, lately practised by men of great knowledge: And now newly enlarged, with divers necessary Phisicke helpes, and knowledge of the names and naturall disposition of diseases, that most commonly happen to men and women. Not impertinent for every good Huswife to use in her house, amongst her owne familie. At London, printed by J R for Edward White, and are to be sold at his shop at the little North doore of Paules, at the signe of the Gunne, 1600, reprinted several times.]

1575: *A PROPER NEW BOOKE OF COOKERY.* Declaring what maner of meates be best in season for al times of the yeere, and how they ought to be dressed, & served at the Table, both for fleshe dayes and Fish daies. with a new addition, very necessary for al them that delight in Cookery. Imprinted at London in Fleet-streete, by William How for Abraham Veale.

1576, 1583: The *FIRST BOOKE OF TABLE PHILOSOPHIE* treateth of the nature and qualitie of all manner meates, drinkes, and Sauces that are used at meales. The *SECOND BOOKE OF TABLE PHILOSOPHIE* which speaketh of the maners, behaviour, and usadge of all sutch with whome wee may happen to be conversaunt at the Table. The *THIRD BOOKE OF TABLE PHILOSOPHIE* which containeth certen delectable and pleasant Questions, to bee propounded for mirth while we be at meate or at any other time. The *FOURTH BOOKE OF TABLE PHILOSOPHIE* which compriseth many merry honest Jestes, delectable devyses and pleasant purposes, to be for delight and recreation at the boord among Company. Written by Thomas Twine, a doctor of Lewes, or Thomas Turswell, a Canon of St Paul's.

1584 and 1591: *A BOOK OF COOKRYE* Very Necessary for all such as delight therin. Gathered by A. W. at London, Printed by Edward Allde.

c. 1585, 1596: *THE GOOD HUSWIFES JEWELL.* Wherein is to be found most excellent and rare Devises for conceites in Cookery, found out by the practise of Thomas Dawson. Whereunto is adjoyned sundry approved receits for many soveraine oyles, and the way to distill many precious waters, with divers approved medicines for many diseases. Also certain approved points of husbandry, very necessary for all Husbandmen to know ... *A Booke of Cookerie.* Newly set foorth with additions, 1596. Imprinted at London for Edward White dwelling at the Little North doore of Paules at the signe of the Gun.

1585, 1597: *THE SECOND PART OF THE GOOD HUSWIFES JEWELL*, Wherein is to bee found most apt and readiest wayes to distill many wholsome and sweete waters. In which likewise is shewed the best manner in preserving of divers sorts of Fruites, and making of Syrropes: With divers Conseites in Cookerie after the Italian and French maner. Never the like published by any untill this present yere, 1585. Imprinted at London for Edward White, dwelling at the little North doore of Paules Church, at the signe of the Gunne.

1588: *THE GOOD HOUS-WIUES TREASURIE.* Beeing a verye necessarie Booke instructing to the dressing of Meates. Hereunto is also annexed, sundrie holsome Medicines for diuers diseases. Imprinted at London by Edward Allde.

1591: *A BOOK OF COOKRYE.* Very necessary for all such as delight therin. Gathered by A. W. And now newlye enlarged with the serving in of the Table. With the proper

Sauces to each of them convenient. At London, printed by Edward Allde, 1591 [see 1544].

1594, 1597: *THE GOOD HUSIFES HANDMAIDE FOR THE KITCHIN.* Containing Many principall pointes of Cookerie, as well how to dresse meates, after sundrie the best fashions vsed in England and other Countries, with their apt and proper sawces, both for flesh and fish, as also the orderly seruing of the same to the Table. Hereunto are annexed, sundrie necessarie Conceits for the preseruation of health. Uerie meete to be adioined to *the good Huswifes Closet of prouision for her Houshold.* Imprinted at London by Richard Jones, 1594 and 1597. [Also there is a version called *The good huswiues Handmaid, for Cookerie in her Kitchin, in dressing all maner of meat, with other wholsom diet, for her and her Houshold, &c.*]

1595: *THE WIDDOWES TREASURE.* Plentifully furnished with sundry precious and approved secrets in Phisicke and Chirurgery, for the health and pleasure of Mankinde. Heereunto are adjoyned, sundrie prittie practices and conclusions of Cookerie, with many profitable and wholsome Medicines, for sundrie diseases in Cattell. At London, printed by J. Roberts for Edward White, 1595.

1596: *THE GOOD HUSWIFES JEWELL.* Wherein is to be found most excellend and rare Deuises for conceites in Cookery, found out by the practise of Thomas Dawson. Wherevnto is adioyned sundry approued receits for many soueraine oyles, and the way to distill many precious waters, with diuers approued medicines for many diseases. Also certain approued points of husbandry, very necessary for all Husbandmen to know. Newly set foorth with additions. 1596. Imprinted at London for Edward

White, dwelling at the litle North Doore of Paules at the signe of the Gun.

1597: *A BOOKE OF COOKERIE*, Otherwise called: The good Huswives Handmaid for the kitchin. Wherein is shewed the order how to dresse meates after sundry the best fashions used in England and other Countries: with their apt and proper sauces both for flesh and fish: as also the orderly serving the same to the Table. Whereunto are annexed sundry necessary Conceites for the preservation of health. London, printed by E. Allde, dwelling in Aldersgate streete, over-against the Pump, 1597. [The headline is 'A New Booke of Cookerie'. See 1594.]

1598: *EPULARIO, OR THE ITALIAN BANQUET*: Wherein is shewed the maner how to dresse and prepare all kind of Flesh, Foules, or Fishes. As also how to make Sauces, Tartes, Pies, etc. After the maner of all Countries. With an addition of many other profitable and necessary things. Translated out of Italian into English. London, printed by A. J. for William Bailey, and are to bee sold at his shop in Gratious street neere Leaden-hall, 1598. [This is a translation of Giovanne de Rosselli's 1516 work.]

1599: *DYETS DRY DINNER*: Consisting of eight severall Courses: 1. Fruites. 2. Hearbes. 3. Flesh. 4. Fish. 5. Whitmeats. 6. Spice. 7. Sauce. 8. Tabacco. All served in after the order of Time universall. By Henry Buttes, Maister of Artes, and Fellowe of C.C.C. in C. ... Printed in London by Tho. Creede, for William Wood, and are to be sold at the West end of Powles, at the signe of Tyme, 1599.

c. 1600, 1602: *DELIGHTES FOR LADIES*, To adorne their Persons, Tables, Closets, and Distillatories; with Beauties, Banquets, Perfumes, & Waters. Reade, Practice, & Censure. At London, printed by Peter Short. Hugh Plat.

1602, 1608: *A CLOSET FOR LADIES AND GENTLEWOMEN*, or, The Art of preserving, Conserving, and Candyng. With the manner howe to make divers kinds of Syrups: and all kind of banqueting stuffes. Also divers soveraigne Medicines and Salves, for sundry Diseases. Entered in the Stationers Registry 1 September 1602 London: Printed by F. Kingston for Arthur Johnson, dwelling neere the great north dore of Paules, 1608.

SECONDARY SOURCE

Brears, Peter, *All the King's Cooks: The Tudor Kitchens of King Henry VIII at Hampton Court Palace* (Souvenir Press, 1999, 2011)

Breverton, Terry, *Breverton's Complete Herbal – A Book of Remarkable Plants* (Quercus, 2011)

Breverton, Terry, *The Physicians of Myddfai: Cures and Remedies of the Medieval World* (Cambria, 2012)

Breverton, Terry, *Breverton's Nautical Curiosities – A Book of the Sea* (Quercus, 2010)

Breverton, Terry, *Everything You Wanted to Know about the Tudors but were Afraid to Ask* (Amberley, 2014)

Dyer, Christopher, *Everyday Life in Medieval England* (Cambridge University Press, 2000)

Hansen, Marianne, 'And Thus You Have a Lordly Dish: Fancy and Showpiece Cookery in an Augsberg Patrician Kitchen', *ACTA*, XXI (State University of New York Press, 1995). [The proceedings of the 1994 Acta conference. This is the first English translation of some recipes from the manuscript written in 1553 by Sabina Welser of Augsburg.]

Hazlitt, William Carew, *Old Cookery Books and Ancient Cuisine* (1902)

Hodgett, Gerald A. J., *Stere Hitt Well. A book of medieval refinements, recipes and remedies from a manuscript in Samuel Pepys' library* (Cornmarket Reprints, 1972)

Loades, David, *The Tudor Court* (Headstart, 1992)

Markham, Gervase, *The English Huswife: Containing the inward and outward Vertues which ought to be in a Compleat Woman – A Work generally approved, and now the Ninth time much Augmented, Purged, and made most profitable and necessary for all men, and the general good* (1615) [Markham's works were updated throughout the seventeenth century, but based in Tudor times.]

Napier, Mrs. Alexander, *A Noble Boke off Cookry ffor a Prynce Houssolde* or eny other estately houssolde (London: c. 1468; reprinted verbatim from a rare MS in the Holkham Collection, 1882)

Plat, Hugh, *Certaine Philosophical Preparations of Foode and Beverage for Sea-men, in their long voyages; with some necessary, approoved, and Hermeticall medicines and Antidotes, fit to be had in readinesse, at sea, for prevention and cure of divers diseases* (1607)

Plat, Hugh, *Sundrie new and Artificiall remedies against Famine* (1595)

Meltonville, Marc, *The Taste of the Fire, The Story of the Tudor Kitchens at Hampton Court Palace* (Historic Royal Palaces, 2007)

Scully, Terence, *Cuoco Napoletano: The Neapolitan Recipe Collection late fifteenth century: A Critical Edition and English Translation* (University of Michigan Press, 2000)

Sim, Alison, *Food and Feast in Tudor England* (The History Press, 1997, 2011)

Spurling, Hilary, *Elinor Fettiplace's Receipt Book* (1604; Penguin repr. 1986)

Trager, James, *The Food Chronology* (New York: Henry Holt & Co., 1995)

Tusser, Thomas, *Five Hundred Points of Good Husbandry* (1557)

Vaughan, William, *Certaine Philosophical Preparations of Foode and Beverage for Sea-men* (1595 and 1607)

Vaughan, William, *Approved Directions for Health, both Natural and Artificial: derived from the best physitians as well moderne as auncient* (1612)

Warner, Richard, *Antiquitates Culinariae Or Curious Tracts Relating to the Culinary Affairs of the Old English* (1791)

USEFUL WEBSITES

Nearly all of the manuscripts and books mentioned in the text have been digitised to be easily downloadable. Of particular excellence and endeavour are the Godecookery, Medievalcookery and Celtnet sites, which give many modern redactions of the above recipes.

medievalcookery.com – this Ohio-based site is absolutely excellent, with hundreds of medieval and Tudor recipes redacted a team of enthusiasts, some with their own websites.

celtnet.org.uk – Dyfed Lloyd Evans' brilliant website for food with 19,300 recipes, ten free historic cookery books and 180 wild foods.

foodsofengland.co.uk – this superb site is attempting to find the story behind every single traditional English dish. There are 3,355 dishes listed, more than 2,500 with the original receipt. It also includes sixty major cookbooks online totalling more than 4 million words, and has food events for each month of the year. Of especial interest are its county dishes.

godecookery.com – the superb website of James L. Matterer, with 500 relevant recipes, but seems to have not been updated for some time.

thousandeggs.com – Cindy Renfrow's website, and this author 'delights in making historic recipe books more widely available to the modern reader for study and re-discovery'. It has links to A Forme of Cury (1390) and Le Ménagier de Paris.

florilegium.org – Stefan's Florilegium, the website of Mark S. Harris (aka Stefan), a fascinating medieval compendium with hundreds of recipes.

coquinaria.nl/english/ – the English version of part of the Dutch website of Christianne Muusers, with recipes throughout history from across the world.

Apologies to any sites omitted. If there is a reprint of this book, I will add them.

As noted above, nearly all the original primary sources above have been digitised, in which you will find more gems of old recipes; for instance, *The Second part of The Good Huswifes Jewell*, can be found at http://quod.lib.umich.edu/e/eebo/ A69185.0001.001/1:3?rgn=div1;view=fulltext.

List of Illustrations

17. Sixteenth-century depiction of a pear. Courtesy of the Rijksmuseum.

18. Sixteenth-century depiction of an apple. Courtesy of the Rijksmuseum.

19. Elizabethan fruit trencher. Courtesy of Jonathan Reeve b2 p734.

20. Sugar cane being prepared. Courtesy of the Rijksmuseum.

21. York bakers at work. Courtesy of Jonathan Reeve b4 p776.

22. York bakers at work. Courtesy of Jonathan Reeve b4 p777.

23. Dodoen's Herbal title page. Courtesy of Jonathan Reeve b5 fp511.

24. Cherries and lemon, sixteenth century. Courtesy of the Rijksmuseum.

25. Sixteenth-century herbal index. Courtesy of Jonathan Reeve b2 p749.

About the Author

Terry Breverton is a former businessman, consultant and academic and now a full-time writer. Terry has presented documentaries on the Discovery Channel and the History Channel. Terry is the author of many books for Amberley on many subjects, including Owain Glyndwr, Richard III, Jasper Tudor, Owen Tudor, Henry VII, Welsh history and the First World War. He lives near Maesycrugiau in Carmarthenshire.

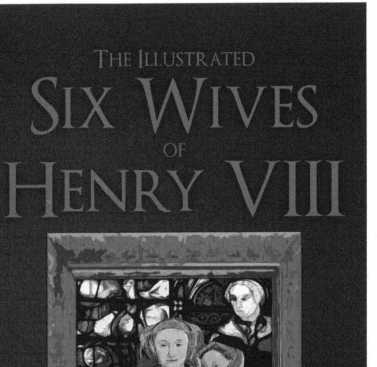